FEELING GREAT IS YOUR NATURAL STATE

A guide to rediscovering and unlocking
the natural joy within

Rick McIlwaine

Copyright © 2021 Rick McIlwaine

Paperback ISBN: 9798531651686

Printed in the United States of America. All rights reserved solely by the author. This book or parts thereof may not be reproduced in any form, stored in a retrieval system, or transmitted in any form by any means - electronic, mechanical, photocopy.

To contact the author, please email: rmcilwaine@live.co.uk

CONTENTS

Introduction..4

Part 1 - Tools for the Body

1. Sleep your way out of stress...................11
2. Breathe new life into yourself....................23
3. Embrace the cold to fire up your day............37
4. Fasting, the ultimate bio-hack......................49
5. Free yourself and your potential by breaking the bonds of addiction......................................63
6. Your brain is like playdough, for you to manipulate..73

Part 1 - Tools for the Mind And Spirit

7. Stay in the Now to transform your life........89
8. Consciousness, your ticket to cloud nine......101
9. Meditation, the single most effective mental tool in your arsenal....................................119
10. Gratitude, saying thank you goes a long way. 131
11. The Law of Attraction: Part 1......................139
12. The Law of Attraction: Part 2......................153

Bibliography..165

INTRODUCTION

Ten years ago, if somebody had asked me would I ever consider writing a self-help book, I would likely have laughed at the idea and ridiculed the very notion, not because I was opposed to the concept of self-help, but rather because I would have been too terrified to do such a thing. Ten years ago, I cared much more about what people thought of me, and I suppose it would be fair to say that I followed a fairly safe, conventional, "don't rock the boat" approach to life. That is no longer the case today.

For the last half-decade, I have been obsessed with the subject of self-improvement and have devoured dozens of books, listened to and watched hundreds of hours of podcasts and lectures. I have personally experimented with each and every technique or practice that I have come across over the years and continue to do so to this day. My passion for continuous self-growth did not appear overnight but has a been a slow-burning development gaining momentum with time, knowledge and experience. I am incredibly thankful for this journey because it is not an exaggeration to say that it has saved my life. In the not-too-distant past, I possessed a tremendous amount of mental baggage, which only very few people were ever aware of. To most people, I probably appeared quite confident and positive, and they were half-right.

As human beings, we are complex things, we don't truly know what lies under the surface of another person's exterior, and I was no different. On the outside, I emanated enthusiasm and confidence, but on the inside, there was a raging typhoon of frustration, self-doubt, bitterness and many other negative emotions. This inner turmoil eventually began manifesting on the outside in the form of cyclical bouts of illness which appeared almost like clockwork, every few months, which went on for years, until I started to take back control.

The negative thoughts and feelings I experienced stemmed from numerous sources, but mainly from physical insecurities and a lack of direction as to what I wanted to do with my life. Now however, I can say that I have completely transformed the way I view myself, the way that I view others and how I view the world. I owe this seismic shift in perception to the discovery and application of a range of tools and techniques that have helped countless others before me and likely many more after me. In this book I will share with you what I believe to be the most powerful, relevant and applicable of these tools.

Over the years, one of many truths which I have come to realise is that the journey of self-improvement is never-ending, there is always a stone left unturned, a shadow that needs illuminated, or a metaphorical weed in the mind to be rooted out, and I find this incredibly exciting. I consider it exciting for the reason that we can always improve in some way, multiple ways even, however we please! It all depends on what you choose to focus on, which leads me to a golden rule to live by, that I shall be repeating throughout this book is, "Where thought goes, energy flows". Simply put, your inner thoughts shape your outer reality, more than you ever would have imagined possible.

Thanks to the internet there is a mind-boggling volume of information on every conceivable topic available today, ready to be mined and extracted by you, whenever you want, wherever you want. We are living in the age of digital information and there has never been a better time to be alive! On the flip-side of the information coin, it is incredibly easy to become overloaded by this tsunami of data, which is why I have strived to include only the most relevant, accurate and actionable material in this book which will help you dissolve stress in your everyday life while at the same time increasing your resistance to stress using methods which will also enhance you physical health as well as your mental health, allowing you to take back control over your mind, body and life, no longer being a victim of your environment or circumstance.

Who is this book for?

This book is for you if you…

- Believe or are open to the suggestion that your thoughts, feelings and action ultimately determine everything in your life.
- Are struggling with self-limiting beliefs or if you find yourself without direction in life and need a helping hand.
- Find yourself plagued by negative thoughts, stress, anxiety etc. You will find great tools within these pages to help you combat these issues which burden far too many people today.
- Feel as if you are drowning under the pressure of trying to "make it" or trying to live up to lofty expectations set by friends, family or society.
- Simply enjoy reading, learning new things about yourself and have a hunger for self-development.

To fully benefit from this book, you will need to go forward from this moment with an open mind, free from prejudice, although a degree of scepticism is always healthy and welcomed.

Why this book needed to be written

Over the years I have consumed more books, podcasts and lectures than I can remember, covering everything from mental and physical health to motivation, inspiration, spiritual development, self-awareness and beyond. Something I came to realise after many months of studying these subjects was that the more books I read and the more interviews I listened to, I noticed that there were many common themes and principles discussed by as many different people, and each person had their own unique viewpoint and experiences with each topic, which meant that there was always something new to be extracted from every book and every discussion.

In March 2020 I was furloughed from my job as an optometrist for a number of months, as were many people across the UK. Not being one for sitting still, I decided to commit myself to unboxing my life's to-do list, to see what I could check-off within the confines of my Belfast city apartment. Within the first fortnight I had well and truly conquered the art of the ice bath, I had gained a tenuous grasp of the skill of Blackjack card-counting, I had reluctantly made the transition from doing barbell bench press to old-school traditional push-ups, which I am now convinced are the ultimate all-in-one home-exercise. But my proudest achievement however was cracking the enigma that is the electronic programming box for my apartment's gas central heating, something I never dreamed I would achieve in this lifetime.

With all of this newfound time on my hands, I soon found myself immersing myself in the world of personal growth and self-improvement world more than I ever had before. I discovered many new podcasts, speakers, scientists, spiritual teachers and authors. All of these enriching experiences ultimately came together, compounded and transformed into something very unexpected. I experienced what is called a spiritual awakening.

It was not long after this before I developed both a burning desire and obligation to share the knowledge and techniques that I had acquired over the months of lockdown-life, in addition to the years of previous study and experience I had acquired throughout university, work and life in general, with the hope of helping others like you to experience the same life-changing benefits which I have been so blessed to experience.

What you will get from this book

Throughout this book you will gain actionable information and tools which will allow you to take back control over the typhoon raging within your mind, enabling you to:

- Recognise stress in your life, increase your resistance to stress and ultimately dissolve it.
- Improve your physical health by burning fat, improving your circulatory system and boosting your immune system, all without having to even lace-up your running shoes.
- Improve your mental health through learning to calm your mind by becoming aware of detrimental thought patterns and self-limiting beliefs.
- Increase your vitality, overcome fatigue, and cultivate commitment with the turn of your shower tap.
- See yourself in a substantially more positive light, allowing you to feel far better about yourself and your life than you ever thought possible.
- Start attracting the people, experiences and things you want into your life.

Part 1 – Tools for the Body

Chapter One

SLEEP YOUR WAY OUT OF STRESS

"Silence is like fertile soil, which acts as it were, awaits our creative act, our seed"

– Arvo Part

Turn off the TV, put your phone on silent, shut out any noise in your immediate environment, and tell me what do you hear? If you tell me that you hear the sound of cars passing by, or your housemate listening to their newest favourite J-rock song, then that unfortunately cannot be helped, but the answer I was hoping for is "silence". Silence is somewhat of a rarity these days, largely due to the fact that we are all almost always "connected" to the outside world through our phones, laptops, tablets, smart TVs, to name just a few.

I recently came across a study carried out at the University of Virginia, where participants were tasked with removing all distractions from their immediate vicinity and to just sit with their thoughts for six to fifteen minutes. The conductors of the study found that 58% of the participants rated the difficulty of this task above the midpoint on the scale (midpoint being "somewhat difficult"), 42% rated their experience below the midpoint (i.e., not overly difficult), and a surprising 32% confessed to looking at their phones during the timeframe.

In a later test within the same study, there was a shocking twist. The subjects were wired up to an electrode which would provide a small but sharp electric shock every time they pressed the button on a small remote control. Each participant had been given a chance to experience a shock beforehand to let them gauge first-hand how painful it was, but despite this, 25% of women 66% of men chose to press the button when they were left to their own thoughts. The essence of these results is that these volunteers preferred to experience pain, rather than be alone with their thoughts.

The trends observed within this study can be seen throughout society today. If you look at ten people waiting at a bus stop, chances are that nine of them are transfixed on their Facebook feed or aimlessly scrolling through Instagram, completely oblivious to their surroundings. Needless to say, it is fortuitous that there are no longer any sabre-toothed tigers roaming the city streets!

Technology is fantastic, and I am in no away opposed to the colossal technological advances in recent years, as life has never been easier. We each have access to more information than we could ever hope to pour through in a lifetime, we can order any item we wish from anywhere in the world and have it delivered to our doorsteps quicker than my 2016 notebook takes to bootup. It has never been easier to stay in contact with friends and family through the medium of social media, but social media in particular, is a double-edged blade.

Is it a coincidence that stress levels, anxiety and depression are at an all-time high with social media becoming an ever-encroaching entity in everyday life? For many people, the first thing they do as soon as they wake up is reach for their phone, scroll through their Facebook newsfeed, check their emails, read some WhatsApp messages, and catch the morning news, which is almost certainly, negative in nature. This routine is almost certainly repeated just before sleep at the end of the day as well, which in a nutshell means that they are starting and ending the day by loading their brains up with negative and depressing clutter.

Life in the fast lane

"The ability to be in the present moment is a major component of mental wellness." – Abraham Maslow

For the vast majority of people in the modern era, stress has become part of daily life. In the UK, 74% of adults felt so stressed at one point in 2018 that they felt overwhelmed or unable to cope, and 20.6% of people have had suicidal thoughts at some point over the previous 12 months, with over one in three 16-24-year-olds having such thoughts. There are over 725,000 people in the UK living with eating disorders and 20% of the population live with depression. While there is a myriad of causes for these bleak statistics, the major underlying denominator by far, is stress.

Like air, for many people, stress is everywhere. It is likely there to some degree in the morning when you are rushing to get yourself in gear for the day ahead, it is probably with you on your way to work like an uninvited passenger. It likely accompanies you throughout the work day in the form of an ear-piercing desk phone ring tone, on the return journey home when the elderly lady is holding up traffic in the over-taking lane whilst tottering along at 50mph, totally oblivious to the world of chaos and vitriol not 10 metres behind her.

This tension then carries over when you return home, in

the form of bickering with your family, housemate, partner, or microwave, which has inconveniently decided to call it quits at the least desirable time. While having a well-earned dinner you decide to catch-up on the affairs of the world by switching to your usual news channel, only to learn of the latest natural disaster, mass murder, or political scandal. After seeing off the last of your potatoes and carrots, you then decide to watch an episode of your favourite soap opera, or perhaps an episode of a gritty murder-mystery, which by themselves appear completely harmless, but think about this.

When have you ever seen an episode of a soap opera have a happy ending, or did not involve at least one horrendously depressing scene? Mentioning no soaps in particular (Eastenders). Then finally before bed, you scroll through your social media accounts and check the final news bulletins of the day before switching off the light and drifting off into a shallow and broken slumber.

Your day may not resemble the day which I have outlined above in any way, but if you look at it through an objective lens, it is not hard to see how easy it is for stress to accumulate throughout your waking hours. You might be wondering, "So what?" and it's only natural to think that a small amount of stress is okay, and that nothing bad will happen to you, until it eventually does, in the form of high blood pressure, insomnia, headaches, infertility, stomach problems, muscle atrophy, anxiety, depression, weakened immune system eventually leading up to an eventual cerebral stroke or heart attack.

A BRIEF OVERVIEW OF WHAT HAPPENS WITHIN THE BODY DURING STRESS

The nervous system is responsible for the coordination of body movement and transmission of electrical impulses between the brain and body. It is a highly complex system and could fill a thousand-page textbook all by itself, but for now, let's keep it simple and concise. There are two main branches to the human nervous system: the central nervous system (CNS) and the peripheral nervous system (PNS)

The CNS is comprised of the brain and the spinal cord. The PNS is comprised of two subdivisions; the somatic nervous system, which consists of peripheral nerve fibres, responsible for detecting sensory information from the peripheral organs, such as your hands and feet, and relaying this information to the CNS. The second division, and the one which we are more interested in is the autonomic nervous system (ANS).

The ANS governs many critical functions within the body, including heart rate, respiratory rate, pupil responses, sexual arousal, and digestion. It is the ANS which controls our fight or flight response and can be broken down into two distinct branches; the sympathetic system which can be regarded as the fight or flight system, and the parasympathetic system as the rest or digest system, both of which are vital for our survival. Another way to visualise the two divisions of the ANS is the sympathetic system as the accelerator pedal of a car and the parasympathetic as the brake pedal.

In our early days as hunter-gatherers, it was this fight or flight response which would come to our aid if we were suddenly threatened by the appearance of a predator. The adrenal medulla within the adrenal glands of the kidneys are stimulated to produce and secrete adrenaline and noradrenaline (aka epinephrine and norepinephrine) which bring about a substantial cascade of changes within the body.

Heart rate quickens, blood pressure increases, the blood vessels in the viscera (internal organs) constrict, which slows down the digestive and urinary systems as these are not regarded by the body as necessary in this moment of life or death. The pupils of the eyes dilate, allowing more light into the eye and the ciliary muscles controlling the lens contract, thinning the lens, and facilitating distance vision, to help you better assess your surrounding environment. The bronchioles within the lungs dilate to allow more oxygen and carbon dioxide exchange to occur, more oxygen facilitates increased respiration, the process which converts glucose and oxygen into carbon dioxide, water, and energy.

Another key compound is released into the bloodstream when you find yourself in a threatening situation, cortisol, also known as the stress hormone. Cortisol is an immunosuppressive steroid hormone also released from the adrenal glands, and in small doses it is actually beneficial to the body in that it temporarily reduces pain sensitivity, heightens memory, and also provides short bursts of energy. Traditionally, this response was intended to provide a short-term physical boost when engaging in physical combat, or when attempting to flee from a predator.

In the current age, however, rarely is there ever actually any physical danger, unless perhaps you are scrambling to move out of the way of a speeding bus! This typical lack of physical danger often means that the recently secreted cortisol is not being properly vented, or released from the blood, resulting in a cortisol build-up, which can have many detrimental effects in the body, including weight gain by fat-retention, increased cholesterol, blood pressure and risk of heart disease. It is also not uncommon to experience impaired cognitive ability including brain fog, memory lapses and learning difficulty due to chronically raised cortisol levels.

ON THE FLIP SIDE

You have likely heard of some incredible feats performed by ordinary people under desperate circumstances. For example, in 2019, a 16-year-old American football player lifted a 1.4 ton or 3000 lb car off his neighbour after getting stuck underneath it. Another example is in 2013, Oregon, where two teenage sisters of 16 and 14 years old successfully lifted a tractor high enough to save their father who had been pinned underneath. Possibly one of the most amazing examples of sudden bursts of superhuman strength can be seen in the story where a five foot zero, 90 pound 41-year-old Canadian mother was able to survive in what could only be described as a brawl with a wild 700-pound polar bear, when it approached her seven-year-old son. She was able to distract the bear long enough and survive several thunderous blows from its colossal paw before a neighbour fired several rifle shots into the air, which successfully scared the bear away.

While it is clear to see that there are huge, life-saving benefits to be gained from tapping into this ancient and powerful system under times of great physical stress, the problem with modern life is that many people are constantly and unconsciously tapping into it. The average person activates their sympathetic nervous system numerous times on a daily basis due to small but accumulative stressors and are not able to down regulate this response, and that is wherein the problem lies, in that stress is always there to some degree, like a persistent stain on a white t-shirt.

Sleep away the stress in your life

There are countless ways of combating stress, but one of the best ways of naturally dissolving it and minimising the impact it has on you and your life, is learning to optimise your sleep. This costs you absolutely nothing to do and you can start taking steps to sleep better right now.

Let me now ask you, how well do you sleep? Does it take a long time for you to drift off? Do you frequently wake up throughout the night? Do you wake up feeling more tired than what you did before falling asleep in the first place? If you answered yes to any of these questions, then it likely that you may benefit from re-evaluating your sleeping practice. When you improve your quality of sleep, you help to reduce your overall level of stress the next day, when you reduce your level of stress, you will sleep better the following night, in effect a positive feedback loop is formed, whose benefits will steadily compound over time!

In addition to the correlation between poor sleep quality and increased levels of stress, anxiety and depression, additional symptoms include but are not limited to impaired memory, reduced cognitive performance, irritability, increased risk of heart disease, muscular aches and pains, and even a greater risk of type 2 diabetes.

Steps you can take right now to transform how you sleep

- **Shut out all light** – the body possesses a biological clock, known as the circadian rhythm. At night time, levels of what we can refer to as the sleep hormone, melatonin begin to rise naturally, preparing you for the land of nod, but when you are exposed to light, be it home interior lighting, car headlights, phones, laptops, etc, this suppresses the release of melatonin, making it more difficult to drift off. Therefore, I strongly recommend you fully close your curtains and/or blinds to block out all sunlight, close your bedroom door, turn out any nightlights, and avoid looking at your phone or laptop for least an hour before bed.

- **Install a blue-light filter on your devices** – this point follows on from the previous one. Blue light is especially disruptive when it comes to affecting melatonin levels, and by extension, affecting your quality of sleep. Harvard researchers have found that blue light can shift the circadian backwards by as much as three hours compared to pure green light, and that it suppresses the rise in melatonin for twice as long. Thankfully, virtually all modern phones, laptops and tablets come with blue light filtering software, and even if they don't it can easily be downloaded from any app store. I downloaded my first blue light filter nearly five years ago, and even if I break my own rule and use my phone before bed, it makes a substantial difference to how easily I fall asleep, but don't take my word for it, try it for yourself and see how it helps you. Blue light filters can also be applied to spectacle lenses, and they are something which I recommend to all of my patients, especially if they are particularly device heavy.

- **Avoid stimulants** – This might seem obvious but try to avoid consuming any caffeinated beverages or alcohol in the final hours of the day. There is debate over what is a suitable window of time to reserve between having a cup of your favourite Columbian blend and when you go to bed, some argue that it should be 4-6 hours, others suggest less, or even more than this. I believe that there is a considerable range from person to person in how they tolerate and process caffeine, and with that being said, I would advise you to listen to your body and do what you feel works best for you.

- **Avoid eating heavy foods** – with this one, you can take it with a pinch of salt! I recommend that you avoid eating any heavy foods or sugary snacks right before bed as it results in your digestive system having to work overtime, making it substantially more difficult to fall asleep. The purpose of food is to supply the body with the ingredients necessary to produce energy, do you need energy to help you fall asleep? On average, having your final bite at least three hours before bed is a widely accepted recommendation, but again, this may vary from person to person, depending on your rate of metabolism.

- **Settle your mind** – if you can quiet your mind when lying in bed at the end of a long day, you will transform your quality of sleep. Take it from someone who once had an extremely restless mind, I used to lie awake for hours running through dozens of random topics in my mind from Star Wars fan theories to what will happen if the Las Vegas reservoir should dry-up as a result of global warming, so as you can see, very random. A quick, easy and effective way to quiet your mind is to simply breath long, slow and deep, following your breath from start to finish. This works because you have shifted your focus from many irrelevant things to a singular focal point. It may take some practice, but you will reap dividends the next day.

Maximising the quality of your sleep can bestow upon you many other amazing benefits in addition to feeling completely rejuvenated the following morning, these include.

- Maintenance of a healthy immune system. Entering a state of deep sleep allows the body's rest and repair mechanisms to work uninterrupted. There have likely been times in your life where you have felt run down due to having experienced greater levels of stress than normal, and it has been these times where illnesses have suddenly manifested themselves, almost overnight, such as aches pains, colds, flus, cold sores etc. The body's immune system is constantly waging a never-ending war against invading bacteria and viruses, it is during states of chronic stress or sleep-deprivation that the immune system falters and balance is upset, resulting in sickness.
  - Improved sense of wellbeing.
  - Improved cognitive ability, attention span and concentration.
  - Improved control of bodyweight and possible reduction in the amount of fat stored in the body, likely due to lowered cortisol levels.
  - Increased lifespan by as much as 15%.
  - Reduced blood pressure and protection against heart disease, cardiovascular disease, stroke and irregular heartbeat.

- Reduced risk of developing diabetes due to a positive influence on blood sugar control.

As you can see, there is a staggering number of benefits to be had from optimising something as simple as your quality of sleep, and the best of it is, it is completely free, and you can do it right now! I am a big fan of sleep myself, and I always aim to get seven hours each night. Most nights, my sleep is deep and full of vivid dreams, even lucid dreams occasionally, which are always a fantastic experience. If you have never had a lucid dream, it is where you are consciously aware of the fact that you are dreaming, which opens up a world of limitless possibilities for the duration of the dream, where you can control almost all aspects of your dream-reality. Unfortunately, there is no sure-fire way of consciously triggering such dreams to occur, but there are techniques available which can increase the chances of having such dreams, but they are quite complex and beyond the scope of this book, but suffice to say, it is a fascinating subject in and of itself.

In essence, having a great night's sleep will lay the foundation for a great day ahead. You have so much influence over the quality of your sleep, all you need to do is realise this truth, take stock in what you do within the hours leading up to sleep, and simply start implementing the steps outlined in this chapter to completely revamp and optimise this vital component of your life.

"Sleep is the golden chain that ties health and our bodies together." – Thomas Dekker

Chapter Two

BREATHE NEW LIFE INTO YOURSELF

"If I had to limit my advice on healthier living to just one tip, it would be simply to learn how to breathe correctly"

– Dr Andrew Weil

Breathing is a fascinating subject, and a vital activity, because if you did not do it, you would not be alive! My question to you now is, how often do you focus on breathing? I mean, how many times a day, week or month do you consciously breath as deeply as you can, and pay attention to the flow of your breath? Don't worry if the answer is rarely, or never, because it is something that you can start doing right now. There are many different breathing methods and styles developed across countless cultures, religions, and peoples, but let's not overwhelm ourselves with more than we need to and keep things simple.

As a keen but very amateur trumpet player and saxophonist, I have a longstanding appreciation for the importance of the breath, if you have never played a brass instrument such as a trumpet, trombone or tuba, then I would highly recommend you try it at least once, just to get a basic idea of how much lung power it takes to even make a simple squeak! Unlike almost all other instruments across all genres of music, brass instruments, and in particular, the trumpet require constant practice, not just to simply be able to play a piece of music, but to maintain the required level of lung power, and embouchure, which is how the lips are used when pressed against the instrument's mouthpiece.

In order to make any sound at all on a trumpet, you must press your lips against the metal mouthpiece, not too hard though, otherwise you will hasten the fatigue of the upper lip muscles, which will result in the dreaded "rubber-lip" syndrome, where the lip is essentially blown out, and can no longer vibrate to produce a sound, resulting in you having to pretend as if you are still playing, while your colleagues pick up the slack (something which has happened to me during gigs, more times that I would care to admit). With the lips pressed against the mouthpiece, you then proceed to buzz through the mouthpiece to make the instrument sing, you do not simply blow, unfortunately. Why not try this yourself right now? Simply press your lips together and blow while keeping them held together. The higher the note that you wish to play, the faster the air stream needs to travel, which is achieved by squeezing your diaphragm and tightening your lips.

There are many benefits to playing any instrument, but there are several specific benefits with brass instruments. I found that after years of practice, I had developed lungs of iron and could easily blow up any rubber balloon I came across, without having to stretch it beforehand, an invaluable skill when it came to birthday parties! I also noticed that after even just several minutes of blowing, I would feel incredibly alert and refreshed. This is due to having to take many successive deep breaths continuously when playing, in addition to constantly squeezing my diaphragm to reach the high notes, which results in my body and in particular my head becoming highly oxygenated, therefore promoting wakefulness.

Breathing in the Real World

My eyes were truly opened to the power of breathing when I discovered the famous Dutch extreme athlete Wim Hof who has developed his own unique method of breathing. Hof developed a unique form of controlled hyperventilation after years of research, trial and error across numerous ancient practices including yoga and tummo. At first the concept of hyperventilating might sound daunting, but his technique has stood up to scientific scrutiny and been proven to be effective in not only reducing stress levels, but also in reducing inflammation throughout the body, improving health, sense of well-being, and even enhancing athletic performance. There are many resources available online published by Hof himself and others like him focusing on this very subject, and I personally encourage you to look into his personal work, as it contains some extremely interesting and beneficial material, a great place to start is at his website www.wimhofmethod.com.

In short, this breathing method involves 3 rounds consisting of 30-40 breaths, each separated by a retention phase after exhalation which is held for as long as is comfortable, and then a subsequent recovery breath which is held for 15 seconds. Begin the first round by inhaling fully, then exhale partially (or as Hof says, "Fully in, then let it go!"), complete this for thirty to forty breaths. You may feel yourself becoming quite light-headed or dizzy, especially during the first few times attempting this technique, which is why you should only ever do it when sitting comfortably or lying down. You may also experience a tingling in your extremities, which is normal, and I will elaborate more on that shortly.

I am aware of how counter-intuitive it sounds in performing a breath hold after exhaling, but you will be surprised at your lack of need to breath, for a much longer time than you would imagine. See for yourself right now. If you exhale and simply hold your breath for as long as you can, you will likely need to take another breath within 20-30 seconds. After completing just one round of this breathing routine, you will very likely be able to hold your breath anywhere from 60 to 90 seconds or even beyond. When you finally feel the need to breath, do just that. Fully inhale and hold for a further 15 seconds, but as you are holding, squeeze your abdominal muscles as if you were bracing your core for doing a squat movement. After this final hold, you have successfully completed the first round, now simply repeat 2 more times and you will have completed your first session. I have included a detailed step-by-step guide to walk you through the process at the end of this chapter.

Part 1 – Hyperventilation

Several physiological changes occur within the body as a result of this breathing technique. Firstly, hyperventilation causes the sympathetic nervous system to become activated, and as know from earlier, this is the body's fight or flight response. This results in adrenaline being released from the kidneys which increases heart rate and redirects blood flow to the major muscle groups.

The amount of oxygen binding to the red blood cells increases slightly from approximately 98% to 99%, while conversely, the level of carbon dioxide in the blood reduces. This reduction in carbon dioxide increases the alkalinity of the blood from 7.4 to approximately 8.0 making it less acidic, or more alkaline, which prevents the activation of nociceptors, the pain receptors within the body, therefore increasing your tolerance to pain for a period of time.

The reduction in Carbon Dioxide, known as hypocapnia leads to a mild constriction of the blood vessels, which gives rise to the tingling pins and needles sensation, described as "intermittent respiratory alkalosis" by the Radboud University Medical Centre. Another effect of the reduced Carbon Dioxide is reduced offloading of oxygen from haemoglobin, or in other words, oxygen is bound more strongly to the red blood cells, temporarily reducing your body's ability to utilise oxygen, this is why it is crucial to perform the technique when sitting or lying down in case you were to pass out.

Part 2 – Retention

The subsequent breath hold phase immediately follows the breathing phase and serves to replenish the Carbon Dioxide lost from the blood during the breathing segment. Oxygen and carbon dioxide levels fall and rise, respectively. Oxygen is consumed by the tissues of the body to fuel respiration, the body's process of producing energy, while carbon dioxide is produced by as a waste product of respiration. The pH level returns to normal about eighty to ninety seconds into the breath hold. It is during this breath hold phase, that the body switches from the sympathetic nervous system to the rest or digest parasympathetic system, and then again towards the end of the breath hold, when you are reaching the limit of how long you can maintain the hold, the body enters a temporary state of hypoxia, as there is not enough oxygen available at the tissue level to allow the body to maintain homeostasis, or equilibrium.

This temporary hypoxic state causes the sympathetic nervous system to be reactivated, releasing yet more adrenaline into the blood stream, but this time something else happens. Hypoxia triggers a glycoprotein called erythropoietin (EPO) to become upregulated, activating a process called erythropoiesis which is the production of red blood cells within the bone marrow. This is very similar to what occurs when marathon runners undergo altitude training, for the purpose of increasing the red blood cell count, which increases how much oxygen their blood can hold at any one time, which by extension means more oxygen is supplied to the working muscles of the body, enhancing stamina and delaying muscle fatigue.

Part 3 – Recovery phase

Finally, after the breath is held for as long as is reasonably comfortable, a singular, deep recovery breath is taken to restore the depleted oxygen levels and also helps the body switch back to the rest and digest, or parasympathetic nervous system.

Traditional medical understanding teaches that the autonomic nervous system cannot be consciously influenced, but that is no longer true. In 2014, this particular breathing routine, the Wim Hof routine went under scrutiny at Radboud University in the Netherlands. Twenty-four healthy, non-smoking Dutch males were exposed to 2 ng/kg of endotoxin E. coli in a hospital setting. Symptoms of an E. coli infection include stomach pains, cramps, diarrhoea, fatigue, nausea, vomiting and fever, so this was not a risk-free walk in the park experiment by any stretch of the imagination. Eighteen individuals were assigned to a group which was to be specifically trained by Hof himself in the breathing method over a four-day period. After completing the training, twelve final participants were chosen to take part in the trial. The remaining twelve were in the control group. The results were conclusive.

Upon exposure to the endotoxin, every one of the trained

individuals successfully suppressed their bodies' innate inflammatory response and remained completely symptom-free, compared to the control group, where all twelve volunteers became ill. The trained men were consciously able to control their ANS which resulted in elevated adrenaline levels and increased presence of interleukin-10 proteins in the blood. These interleukin-10 proteins are anti-inflammatory cytokines, which along with adrenaline help to dampen the innate inflammatory response. Furthermore, elevated adrenaline levels are known to stimulate leucocytosis, which is the production of white blood cells, including leukocytes, monocytes, lymphocytes and neutrophils in the hours following exposure to this particular endotoxin when compared to the control group which did not experience any similar rise in adrenaline. This means that the immune systems of the trained individuals were able to respond much more effectively to the invading bacteria while at the same time exhibiting a substantially lessened inflammatory response, which is responsible for the fever-like symptoms.

A particularly interesting benefit – nasal decongestion

Since my early childhood, I have had irritable sinuses, a trait I inherited from my dad, along with his questionable sense of humour and passion for percentages and decimals. Rarely would I venture out from the house without a handkerchief in my pocket, in fact, if I could only have taken a handkerchief or my phone when leaving the house for a few hours, I would take the handkerchief, for fear of my nose betraying me and blocking up. During the first few months practicing this breathing technique, I was inhaling and exhaling through my mouth, as I found it easier to keep up the brisk pace.

One day, I decided to try and breath in through my nose for the first round. It was more difficult than breathing through my mouth, but I persevered to the end of the round, then did the breath hold as normal. As soon as I began the second round, my mind was blown. My nose was completely clear, the clearest it had ever been in my life up to that point. I believe that this surprising but welcome benefit is a further side-effect of the elevated adrenaline levels, as adrenaline is known to have airway-dilating properties, hence it's use as an anaphylactic treatment. Another welcome benefit is found in the release of a unique signalling molecule known as nitric oxide. Nitric oxide is released within the lining of the nasal passage, and causes vasodilation, or widening of blood vessels, which ultimately improves circulation around the body, which enhances mental clarity, wakefulness and physical performance.

BREATHING MORE DEEPLY THROUGHOUT THE DAY.

By taking over 90 consciously deep breaths over three separate rounds first thing in the morning, every single day for almost a year now, I have found that this spills over into my breathing throughout the day. You will become much more mindful of your breath from morning to night, if I feel my stress levels rising at any point, I almost automatically breath more slowly and deeply for at least one minute, preventing the stress hormone cortisol from rising and putting a dampener on the day.

BETRAYED BY A KIWI

While not performed in as scientific a setting as the Radboud University experiment discussed above, I have gained my own insights into potential benefits obtained through controlled hyperventilation. All my life, I have known that I am allergic to peanuts and Brazil nuts, but as far as foodstuffs are concerned, that is it. While visiting home one weekend, I decided to treat myself to the juicy nectar of a golden-ripe kiwi, as I have done countless times previously in my life. I cannot explain what happened, but I experienced a mild allergic reaction, similar to that which I would have experienced had I eaten a peanut, albeit significantly less serious thankfully.

My lips began tingling and swelling, and my throat was starting to get irritated, I can thankfully say that I did not feel the same bone-chilling impending doom I would have experienced had it been an actual peanut, but this was still far from pleasant. I would also like to emphasise that my nut allergy is mild relative to other allergy sufferers, as in I thankfully have never needed to carry and epi-pen or receive treatment from one. After devouring the kiwi, it was not long before I felt the familiar biological cascade gather momentum, when almost instinctively I began the controlled hyperventilation routine I had done every morning for many months, because I knew that it would flood my blood with adrenaline, the very same adrenaline that is administered to a person via an epi-pen when experiencing anaphylaxis. After completing thirty to thirty-five breaths, I began the breath hold, and held it for almost three minutes, then completed the first lap with a fifteen second inhale, hold and abdominal squeeze.

After completing just one entire round of the breathing regimen, the creeping allergic reaction was completely and utterly neutralised. Gone without a trace! This has happened numerous times since then, when I have attempted to eat a kiwi (one of my favourite fruits and I refuse to give them up) and every time, one complete round of breathing nips any discomfort in the bud, amazingly quickly too. I am not brave (or stupid) enough to attempt this with a peanut, as it would be an unnecessary and reckless risk, but I can personally testify that there seems to be a strong anti-allergy response to this breathing method. Please don't take this as fact or medical advice however, as what works for me, may not work for everyone, but if you ever do find yourself experiencing mild anaphylaxis, and you do not have an antihistamine or epi-pen available, then this could be a viable alternative.

SUMMARY OF KEY BENEFITS YOU MAY EXPERIENCE WITH THIS BREATHING ROUTINE:

- Increased alertness and focus due to the release of adrenaline.
- Increased pain threshold (temporary) due to the increased alkalinity of the blood and inactivation of pain receptors.
- Increased fat loss due to stimulation of both sympathetic and parasympathetic nervous systems as links have been made in studies between autonomic nervous system dysfunction and reduced fat metabolism.
- Boosted immune system function due to increased numbers of white blood cells.
- Improved cardiovascular fitness due to increased numbers of red blood cells and therefore elevated oxygen-binding capacity.
- Reduced inflammation due to release of anti-inflammatory cytokines.
- Nasal decongestion, due to the general anti-inflammatory effects of adrenaline throughout the body and the release of vasodilating nitric oxide from the epithelial lining of

the nasal pathway.
- Dampening or even suppression of allergic reactions due to the release of adrenaline.

EXERCISE TO TRY AT HOME

This routine can be done in the morning, afternoon, evening, or anytime you are feeling particularly stressed, but do not do it when driving, if you are about to drive, or when in the bath or shower, as with many breathing exercises, there is a chance you may become light-headed, or in severe cases, lose consciousness. This is where common-sense comes into play. A small degree of light-headedness can be expected when performing this routine, especially the first few times that you do it.

LEVEL ONE BREATHING ROUTINE

1. **Set-up:** Find a quiet space where you will not be disturbed and either sit down or lie down. This can be done in complete silence, or you may want to have a gentle soundtrack to help you focus. I like to play a nature scene on Youtube on my smart TV where there are many fantastic examples to choose from.
2. **Breathe:** When you are ready to begin, fully inhale through either your mouth or nose, then exhale partially. By partially if you inhale 100% then exhale about 70-80%, i.e., not a complete exhalation.
3. **Repeat:** Repeat this cycle at a reasonably brisk pace for thirty to forty breath cycles.
4. **Breath hold:** On the final breath cycle, simply exhale as you have been doing throughout the round and hold. This is now the breath retention phase. Hold your breath for as long as you are comfortable with,

the length of the breath hold is not crucial, but for a ballpark I would recommend aiming for 60 seconds, 90 seconds and 120 seconds for the first, second and third rounds, respectively.
5. **Recovery breath**: When you need to breath, fully inhale and hold the air in your lungs for fifteen seconds, while squeezing your abdominal muscles at the same time, this helps return oxygenated blood to the head, relieving any light-headedness. You have now completed one complete round.
6. **Repeat three more times.**
7. **Have a fantastic day.**

Level Two breathing routine

This is the version which I use each and every day, within ten minutes of having my cold shower and before breakfast. This breathing routine is exactly the same as in the standard version outlined above, the difference lies in what you do during the breath hold, or retention phase. With an overwhelming number of self-help and meditative practices available at the end of any google search, and with there being a limited amount time to spare in the morning before work, I have developed a routine which combines several different practices into one concise package, utilising the benefits of breathing, mindfulness, positive affirmations, meditation and visualisation. This routine has been the rock which I have built each and every day upon for the last year, and its effects seem to get stronger and stronger the more that I do it.

1. Complete each breathing round as outlined in the level one breathing routine.
2. During the breath hold for each cycle, pick and perform one of the following.

a. Close your eyes and be mindful to the moment and your environment. If you are listening to a nature track, pay close attention to the sounds that you hear, and do not judge or pass opinion on what you hear, simply be aware of it.
b. Keep your eyes open and pick a point on the nature scene on your tv, if you are using a tv, otherwise, simply pick a specific point on the wall, or if you are outside, perhaps a tree branch for example. By focusing on a point of singularity, you calm the clatter within your mind. Again, do not think about what it is you choose to focus on, simply observe it without judgement.
c. Close your eyes and proceed to give thanks for everything you have in your life, and for each thing you are thankful for, pause slightly and think why you are grateful for it and generate feelings of gratefulness for each thing you think of. This is an outstandingly effective way of priming your mind and body for having a terrific day, simply because a state of gratitude is a state of abundance. We shall focusing more on the power of gratitude in chapter ten.
d. Close your eyes and set your intentions for the day, week, month, year or beyond. This is in essence, goal setting, but something you can do each and every day. Decide how you want your day, week, month or year to unfold. Visualise in your mind exactly how many sales you want to make at work, or how you intend to interact with your colleagues, or how you intend to set a new personal best in the bench press, and specifically, what weight. See your intentions in your mind's eye, feel what it would be like to achieve your target, then let it go and think

no more of it for the rest of the day. These principles underlie what is known as the Law of Attraction, which will be explored in much more detail in chapter eleven.
3. Have an even more fantastic day.

Chapter Three

EMBRACE THE COLD TO FIRE UP YOUR DAY

"If we always choose comfort, we never learn the deepest capabilities of our mind or body"
– Wim "The Iceman" Hof

It is probably safe to say, that the vast majority of people enjoy a piping-hot shower first thing in the morning, and there is nothing wrong with that at all. As you will probably agree, one of the worst things that can happen in the morning is when you are enjoying the glorious comfort of that lovely warm shower, when all of a sudden, without warning, it runs cold, and you suddenly have a new found appreciation for what Jack must have experienced back in 1912 when Rose didn't move over to let him onto the giant door which arguably could have supported the both of them that fateful night when the Titanic sank. Back on point, the general consensus is that a warm shower is good, and a cold shower is unpleasant.

All of us have been conditioned by modern society to pursue comfort at all costs, if it gets too cold, you put on a coat, if it gets too warm, you turn on the air-conditioning, you could even compare it to your very own bio-thermostat. You are trained from a young age to avoid discomfort wherever possible, I want to tell you, that this is a terrible philosophy and one which may even have disastrous repercussions on both your physical and mental health. Think of astronauts who spend prolonged periods of time in space. After spending just five to eleven days in zero gravity, astronauts can lose up to twenty percent of their muscle mass due to lack of stimulation, which is usually supplied by the force of gravity. When they return to earth, everything is substantially more difficult, simple tasks such as climbing stairs, walking and even just standing are significantly more difficult, due to the loss of muscle power.

Resistance strengthens you; it toughens you. When you go to the gym and lift weights, you break down muscle fibre, but only when you really start exerting yourself, the more reps you do, or the more weight you use, the more muscle fibres you recruit. These microtears in the muscle regrow over the following hours and days, resulting in the muscle increasing in size, density and strength, helping you to overcome the challenge should you face it again, this is called muscle hypertrophy and is a fantastically useful evolutionary tool.

The same phenomenon can be seen on a societal scale. As a trend, the richer and more sophisticated a society becomes, the less resistance it experiences. For example, in days gone by, walking or cycling were the predominant modes of transport for most people, whereas now, almost everyone has access to a car. Likewise, in the not-too-distant past, food, let alone junk food was not nearly as readily available as it is today, therefore people had to conserve what they had, and work even harder to obtain it in the first place.

There is an over-abundance of food today, particularly sugary, low protein food and this is especially true in the western world, which unfortunately is fuelling several crises, such as the obesity and diabetes pandemics. In essence, the richer and more comfortable a society becomes, the softer it becomes, and by extension, weaker. It happened to the Romans, it happened to the British Empire, and it is now happening throughout the western world today. Thankfully, you do not need to subject yourself to discomfort all the time to gain substantial benefits. As far as cold exposure is concerned, as little as thirty to ninety seconds each day is enough to gain all the benefits, which we will explore right now.

Boosted immunity

Despite what you may have been led to believe over the course of your life, the cold does not make you sick, it can however suppress the immune system in those who are already sick with for example a cold or flu, possibly making them even more vulnerable to further infection. In healthy individuals, the cold is a powerful training stimulus which strengthens and conditions the immune system, much like how dumbbells and barbells strengthen the musculoskeletal system. A study which can be found in the European Journal of Applied Physiology and Occupational Physiology showed that over time, repeated cold-water exposure increased the total number of white blood cells in the blood, which protect you against illness and disease.

Enhanced circulation within the cardiovascular and lymphatic systems

The human body has approximately 77,000 miles of blood vessels, including arteries, veins, and capillaries, that is almost the same distance as walking around the earth's equator, twice. Surrounding each and every vessel is smooth muscle which contracts and relaxes outside of our conscious control. When exposed to the cold, these smooth muscles squeeze the vessels in the extremities, thus reserving blood and heat for the vital core organs, just think of frost bite as an extreme example of this. It is thought that repeated exposure to the cold trains this smooth muscle tissue to become stronger and more effective, aiding blood circulation, in turn making the cold easier to tolerate, boosting your ability to thermoregulate, or maintain your ideal body temperature.

Not only is the circulation of the cardiovascular system enhanced, but so too is that of the lymphatic system. The lymphatic system runs alongside the main vascular (or circulatory) system of arteries, veins and capillaries, and its purpose is to clear waste products from the body's cells. Unlike the circulatory system which has the heart, the lymphatic system does not have a centralised pump to pump the lymph through the vessels, instead it relies on the contraction of muscles to push the lymph through the vessels throughout the body. If the body does not move enough or if the lymphatic system becomes underactive or slow, the fluid lymph cannot clear away the cellular toxins, which accumulate over time and can manifest as colds, flus, aches, pains and potentially other infections or diseases. When exposed to the cold, the lymph vessels strongly contract, which forces the lymph around the body, flushing out all of the waste as it circulates the body.

Lose weight by creating calorie-burning brown fat

In addition to this vascular workout, another incredible change happens within the body when repeatedly exposed to the cold over time, and that is the conversion of white fat to brown fat. In a nutshell, white fat is metabolically inert "bad fat", and brown fat is metabolically active "good fat". Now let's drill down into these two different types of fat tissue in slightly more detail.

White fat is the one which most of us try to avoid, or lose, as it is a result from surplus calorie intake. White fat cells (or adipocytes) store unspent energy in the form of a large, singular oily droplet, stored just underneath the skin and around the internal organs (subcutaneous and visceral fat respectively) and an excessive build-up of the latter can be particularly dangerous, in the form of heart disease. This white fat is associated with increased levels of the female sex hormone oestrogen and also tends to produce a hunger-stimulating effect. Despite the negative effects of this type of fat, it plays a key role in regulating the body's temperature by providing a layer of insulation under the skin and around the inner organs.

On the other side of the fat-coin there is the metabolically active brown fat. Unlike the inert white fat, each of these cells or adipocytes contains mitochondria (think of these as the powerhouses of the cell), and exist in large numbers of small oily droplets, rather than a single large droplet as with the white adipocytes. Due to their metabolically active nature, each brown fat cell generates heat as it burns calories to produce energy, which also helps to regulate the body's temperature, without shivering (non-shivering thermogenesis). The location of this fat varies somewhat between individuals but is usually most concentrated in the neck, shoulder, and chest regions. An incredible discovery recently revealed that repetitive exposure to the cold can actually convert white fat into brown fat, turbocharging the process of "losing weight" or "burning fat" due to the calorie-burning nature of brown fat cells.

Commit to the cold and see your life radically change

"Commitment is the little choices made every day that lead to the final results we're striving for." – Anonymous

As a civilisation, things have never been so good, our lives our incomprehensibly easier compared to what they were even just one hundred years ago. It does not take a substantial effort to achieve a fantastic level of comfort and convenience in the form of having a warm and secure home, running water, car, internet, mobile phone, more clothes than you can ever wear, large screen 4k TV, a fridge full of food, games consoles, social life and recreational activities such as an annual holiday, trips to the cinema, bowling alley, restaurants, bars, etc. We have grown accustomed to luxury, comfort, and immediate gratification. Many would rather order a book online and have it delivered to their doorstep in 24 hours than take a trip to their local bookshop. There has never been so much choice and availability in the way of sweet, sugary treats and fast food, which is a substantial factor in the global obesity pandemic of which we are currently in the midst of.

By and large, most people will do almost anything to avoid discomfort, examples include having a hot shower, rather than a cold one, cranking up the AC or central heating if we feel a bit warm or chilly, respectively. We constantly bundle ourselves up in layers when venturing outside, even if it is not in fact cold, more often than not. The problem that lies herein is that we have established very narrow and defined parameters, within which we operate our entire lives.

Cultivate discipline and commitment

When you consciously make the decision to expose yourself to the cold, you have already made a huge leap forward, by going beyond your comfort zone. If for example you choose to have a cold shower, or climb into a cold bath, your immediate reaction is to panic, and the body begins shivering in an attempt to generate heat. Overcoming that survival response and panic takes willpower and resolve. To repeatedly do this over time takes discipline. When you develop discipline in this task, it will spill over into other areas in your life (pardon the pun) such as getting up that bit earlier in the morning to fit in that gym routine you always wanted to start, or perhaps it could be you find yourself being more disciplined in what food and drink you put into your body.

Enhanced tolerance to stress

Furthermore, arguably the greatest benefit you get from cold exposure, is the ability to down-regulate the stress response. If you are able to climb into a tub of cold water and get your body to adapt and relax, you immerse yourself in the present moment. When in the present moment, you are not thinking about the next mortgage payment, or that presentation you have to give two weeks from Tuesday, you are not thinking about that irritating client you dealt with 6 hours earlier, there is only the here and now, the cold. Being present is also a powerful meditation and we will explore this further later on in the book, but the key point right now is that if you are able to handle and down-regulate the stress experienced when having a cold shower or bath, this increases your resilience to the stressors of everyday life. You will find that you have almost a metaphorical suit of armour around you at all times, and even if something finds a gap in this armour and cuts you (metaphorically of course) you will recover substantially quicker than you would have otherwise done prior to your cold training.

How I have benefitted from the cold and what you too may experience

I firmly believe that your morning routine can have a substantial impact on how your day will unfold. If you start your day off on the right foot, you will find that most other things almost magically fall into place. Obviously, there is no morning routine or magical practice you can do which guarantees a perfect day every day, because this isn't Disneyland, but you most definitely can stack the odds in your favour, by incorporating practices into your routine such as cold showers and the breathing routine outlined in the previous chapter.

1. **Substantially fewer sick days.** Despite being physically fit and strong my entire life, (of which I largely attribute to my childhood obsession of what is arguably the world's most iconic anime, Dragon Ball, which strongly promotes the values of continually improving yourself, breaking limits and many other invaluable life-lessons) I got sick quite a lot. In particular, from the ages of 20 to 23, I used to get sick like clockwork, in fact I kept a journal of sick days, symptoms and duration. There was a trend. Over the three years, I developed mild flu-like symptoms every seven weeks, which lasted up to ten days a time.

   While not a full-blown flu, it was infuriating and almost depressing, because it made everything difficult. It would always begin with a tender throat as a warning sign, then within 24 hours, I felt like my energy had been cut in half, my head was light, and appetite diminished. I had several blood tests performed at my GP's office, which revealed nothing. My dad even paid the bill for a complete blood work-up at a private healthcare company, which revealed nothing, other than elevated IgE levels, which was not surprising as I had several allergies as a child and still currently have a peanut allergy. I was in perfect health. My diet was clean, my body fat was 8%, and I only drank socially. This recurring mystery illness made no sense whatsoever.

One day after finishing the washing up, I suddenly felt the all-too familiar raw sensation in my throat (this was always the first warning sign), I checked my log of sick days, and sure enough, several weeks had passed since my last bout, it was happening again. I could feel the despair and frustration building inside me. I don't know what made me do what I did next, but I decided to pour a pint of cold water from the tap and chugged it in one go. Like magic, the increasingly tender throat sensation disappeared almost immediately, and the flu-like symptoms did not manifest! After years of getting nowhere, I had finally found a silver bullet to my ailment. Despite never feeling particularly thirsty, my body seemed to experience dehydration, without showing any symptoms at all, other than creating flu-like symptoms on a seven-weekly basis. To this day, I still do not know any more than that.

After discovering the miracle cure that was drinking much more water throughout the day (I always did drink water rather than fruit cordial and soft drinks, but apparently, I needed more than what I was previously getting), I experienced substantially fewer episodes of this mystery illness. Probably closer to one episode every sixteen weeks or more, compared to every seven weeks, I would still get the occasional head cold as well, as is perfectly normal. However, since practicing the previously discussed breathing routine and taking frequent cold showers for almost a year, I have not been sick once. I am not saying that this method will guarantee you perfect health indefinitely, I can only speak on behalf of myself, but I can saw with conviction that these two practices alone have without doubt bolstered both my physical and mental health.

2. **Caffeine-free energy**. Previously, I, like almost everybody, was not a normally functioning human being until I had consumed at least one cup of Columbia's finest roast first thing in the morning. Coffee was my morning elixir, and afternoon elixir... and more often than not, my evening elixir. Needless to say, I drank my fair share of coffee. I still indulge in my morning coffee, but no longer out of necessity, rather, for the enjoyment of its flavour and soothing aroma. After standing under what feels like freezing cold water for ninety seconds, I feel like I'm ready to go to war, with my mental alertness and clarity at raised to an incredible level.

3. **Healthier, less dry hair and skin**. While a more cosmetic benefit than a life-changing one this is still a welcome benefit, nevertheless. When you shower with warm water, the heat strips the hair of many of its essential oils, drying it out and even making it greasy and brittle over time. Cold water prevents this and can even enhance the health and

appearance of both hair and skin, possibly staving off the effects of aging to a small degree as well.

I will not pretend that adapting to the cold was easy for me, because it was not. The very first time I attempted cold water exposure was simply by dipping my hands and feet into just six inches of cold bathwater, and it stung! For the first few days, I could barely keep my extremities submerged for longer than twenty seconds at a time, but as with all things, my perseverance paid off. By the end of the first week of cold-water exposure, I was able to sit in eight inches of cold water for up to five minutes! I will not sugar coat it, but I yelped every time I entered the water, thankfully my determination to condition myself pushed me onwards, this is where self-control and discipline played a huge role. After just a few minutes, my submerged skin turned red, and it felt as if hundreds of tiny needles were piercing my skin.

Over the next few weeks, I had reached the point where I could fill the bath to near the brim and stay within the freezing embrace of the water for over ten minutes, and my skin no longer turned red! My body had finally adapted to the ten-degree Celsius water, as had my mind, for I was able to overcome the trepidation of entering the water more easily each and every time that I did it. This was to become my evening routine for many months before I started adding one to two bags of ice to further increase the difficulty of the challenge.

After approximately nine months of this routine, I felt as if I had mastered the ice bath and began reducing the frequency of which I took them, mainly as it was costing me a surprisingly large amount of money keeping the ice supply flowing, not to mention the local shop could not keep up with my demand. As

I tapered off the cold baths, I began switching to cold showers in the morning, which I find to be more enjoyable and just as beneficial as the baths.

Exercise to try

Begin with your regular warm shower in the morning as usual, but at the very end, turn the temperature to as cold as it can go. You can do this in one go, or you can do it gradually, the choice is yours, but once the temperature has bottomed out, stand in it for thirty seconds the first time you do it, breathing deeply the entire time. I recommend taking several deep breaths just before you make the switch from hot to cold, to help prepare you for the initial jolt. After thirty seconds are complete, simply turn off the shower as normal, exit the shower and take note of how alive and energised you now feel!

As you do this more often, I recommend increasing the time you spend under the cold water. You can add fifteen seconds each day, or you can add thirty seconds, it is completely up to you. Personally, I find a maximum duration of ninety seconds to be the sweet spot, anything beyond this feels to be in the area of diminishing returns, at least from my experience.

Finally, I would advise you not to do this if you feel like you may be coming down with a cold or flu, for the reason that this is an exercise targeting the immune system, subjecting it to a short bout of controlled stress. If you are on the verge of illness, this could push you over that edge, so for that reason, I would recommend using your own judgement, or consult your personal physician.

Chapter Four

FASTING, THE ULTIMATE BIO-HACK

"Instead of looking outside of ourselves and counting potential enemies, fasting summons us to turn our glance inward, and to take the measure of our greatest challenge: the self, the ego, in our own eyes and as others see us"

– Tariq Ramadan

There are few culinary experiences in this world that can beat the sensation of sinking your teeth into a succulent, fresh-cut fillet steak, done blue! Admittedly, I only discovered the joy of blue steak at the age of 29, when out for my brother James' birthday dinner in the Galgorm castle restaurant just outside my mum's hometown of Ballymena. While debating what we would order when the waitress returned, I declared that I would opt for the 14 oz fillet steak, medium rare, and that is when James dropped the gauntlet and dared me to order my steak, but blue. I had never had a blue steak before, but I was all too aware that all that separated it from a raw slab of meat was about fifteen seconds on a hot pan. I reluctantly accepted the challenge, but truthfully, I was devastated, because I had been looking forward to that steak all day.

When the steak finally came, after its several second stint on the pan, it looked like a regular well-done steak on the outside, but as soon as I cut into it, a torrent of pinkish-red blood oozed out from its tender body, I felt ill. My mum said, "Don't eat it, send it back!" to which I replied, "No, this is my fate, I must accept it". Up to this point in my life I had never had a steak less well done than medium-rare, so this was quite a jump for me. As soon as I put that first piece of bloody meat in my mouth, I was converted to the blue club. I had never imagined a steak could taste so good, the texture, the succulence and flavour were collectively almost overwhelming. Had I not stepped outside my comfort zone; I could very possibly have gone the rest of my life having missed out on this amazing jewel.

TEN BUCKS

Several years ago, my brother and I made a pact. The pact was that if one of us dared the other to complete a challenge, the recipient of the challenge must accept it when the gauntlet has been dropped, or face shame, ridicule, and loss of honour. The power of the dare is a double-edged sword however, because the rules stipulate that anyone within the pact who makes a dare, must be prepared to receive a dare, or be caste out of the agreement. The rules are simple, we cannot deliberately dare one another to do something that would likely result in them getting assaulted, arrested, or that might cause harm to anyone or anything. The original purpose of the dares was solely to provide amusement for the giver of the dare, but after having completed more than I can count over the years, I came to realise that they did so much more than provide mere comic relief.

Let me back-up a little bit further to provide some more background context. My former university housemate and good friend Scott stumbled upon an American sitcom, Ed, which follows the lives of two life-long friends, Ed, and Mike, who grew up to be a lawyer and medical doctor, respectively. In virtually every episode there is at least one instance where Ed or Mike dares the other to do some kind of ridiculous challenge. If you have never seen it, I recommend it if you are in the mood for some classic light-hearted American comedy.

After having discovered this comedy jewel, Scott and I have done and still continue to do dares, at the most random of times, one example being years ago when we were passing through Belfast's botanical gardens one summer's day when we came across a small group of attractive young women sitting on the freshly cut grass. Without warning, Scott whispered to me "Ten bucks to walk over to those girls, do a forward roll and simply say, "Ladies", then tip the peak of my non-existent cap". It was a brilliant, but awful dare. I have always been quite shy around girls, so this was a genuinely difficult challenge, or at least it would have been had I paused to consider what I was about to do, fortunately I did not. It was over in a matter of seconds, and in that time my adrenaline went from zero to 100 in no time!

Another great example of a dare occurred when my cousin David and I were engaging in a duel of ten pin bowling at the local Belfast bowling alley one Friday night. We had bowled together a few times previously, and David had never won a game against me (and I intended to keep it that way). Well as fate would have it, in our second game of the night, David had begun to pull ahead several frames into the game, and by the seventh frame, I was beginning to fear for the safety of my winning streak. Suddenly, a moment of divine inspiration flashed into my mind, and just as David was preparing for what could very well have been a turkey (three consecutive strikes),

I dropped the gauntlet once more and said, "Ten bucks if you bowl the rest of the game with your left hand!". All credit to my cousin, he threw away the opportunity to seize glory in what would have been a triumphant victory, to avoid the shame of having broken the covenant of the dare. Needless to say, he was not pleased with me, but more importantly, my record was intact.

Possibly the simplest but most gut-wrenchingly hilarious dare to date occurred several years ago when David and I were having lunch in an American diner in Belfast. We had been seated and given menus by one of the waiters, after a few minutes of deliberation we had decided what we would order. David had chosen a house favourite, the Big Buppa burger, and I chose the Chicago grill chicken. This is when I saw a golden opportunity. I said to my unfortunate cousin, "Ten bucks…" and his face went pale (This was the standard procedure by which every dare was initiated). I then dropped the gauntlet by laying down the following challenge, "Ten bucks, if you say to the waiter when he comes back, and you only say, Big Buppa me." He glared at me across the table because he knew that after all of our previous dares, he could not refuse this challenge, and the colour soon returned to his ashen face.

It was not long before a server returned to take our orders, unfortunately for poor David it was not the original waiter, but rather a very attractive young waitress who looked like she could have been an American football team cheerleader! His face was beetroot before she even spoke. She asked us if we were ready to order, and I was more than happy to oblige and order first, she then turned to David, who without looking up from his menu, croaked the words, "Big Buppa me." The waitress looked a bit confused at this strange request and replied, "Sorry sir, could you repeat that please?" David then looked up to meet her gaze, and repeated his order, with a hint more conviction too, "Big Buppa me." At this point, I had to turn away and look out the window, because tears were streaming down my face. It was all that I could do to contain the volcanic laughter wanting to explode out of me.

While looking away, I then heard the very patient waitress ask, "Does that mean that you want me to bring you a burger?" then after what seemed an eternity, the most awkward silence I have ever experienced was broken by the three golden words, "Big Buppa me." At this point I was on the verge of losing consciousness, never before had I tried so hard to contain such a storm of laughter. Thankfully for all of us, the waitress must have decided that my cousin was a little bit special and thanked him for his order. She then asked what drinks we would like, I ordered a glass of water for myself and then tentatively she looked again to David, who at this point looked like he had planted his face in a pool of crimson paint, "And you sir?" he immediately looked across the table to me with utter panic and pleading in his eyes, "He'll take a Coke." I quickly replied.

After the waitress took her leave, David declared that that was one of the most exhilarating things he had ever done, and that he felt a tremendous surge of adrenaline, as if he were performing a bungee jump, and I could relate all too well, from my own previous experiences of the ten-buck dare. He felt like he had achieved something, as if he had a won competition. As far as his body's chemistry was concerned, he had. He had just experienced a surge in adrenaline, due to the exhilarating experience that had just occurred, once the experience was over and the adrenaline had started to subside, his brain's reward pathway was stimulated, causing the feel-good hormone dopamine to be released, due to his sense of achievement in stepping out of his comfort zone, conquering his fear, putting his ego aside and completing the dare to the end.

Over the last five or so years I have received many and given many dares, mostly with Scott, my cousin David and brother James, I will not elaborate on any more of them in this book, to spare us all the unnecessary humiliation. Despite how ludicrous and even juvenile the concept of dares may appear on the surface, when you analyse it more deeply or better yet, experience doing one for yourself, you will find that there is much more than meets the eye.

Fulfilling an embarrassing dare forces you out of your comfort zone, and it is outside the comfort zone where growth occurs. Nothing remarkable is ever done from a place of comfort, just think of the cold showers. When stepping out of your comfort zone, you are forced to set aside your pride, or your ego, the little voice in your head which tells you that you can't do this, and that you should just remain invisible, and safe. Performing these dares also teaches you that you can summon courage as and when you need it, and after the dare has been completed, you are still standing, albeit possibly slightly red in the face!

FASTING FORCES YOU OUT OF YOUR COMFORT ZONE

Let us now shift our focus back to the main theme of this chapter, fasting. You may be familiar with the concept of fasting, or perhaps not, but here we will explore what fasting is exactly, a variety of approaches as to how it can be done safely and ways in which you can directly benefit from fasting and change your life for the better. Simply put, fasting is the conscious elimination of the intake of food, drink, or both, for a period of time. Some people do it for cultural reasons, some for religious reason, but many today are doing it for the plethora of health benefits that can be gleamed from this ancient practice.

Food has never been so readily available in the history of mankind, than it has in the modern age. Our ancestors would have spent the majority of their time, foraging for food, hunting wild animals, carrying them home to skin them and prepare them, all before they could take a single bite. Today, we can eat whatever we want, as much as we want, whenever we want. Unfortunately, as we all know too well, that this readily available limitless abundance of any and all foods has come with a heavy price. Skyrocketing rates of obesity, diabetes, and heart disease, to name a few of the biggest problems. Diabetes alone for example in the United States has surged from a prevalence of 0.93% in 1958 to 10.3% in 2020, which is approximately 34.2 million people. A further 88 million are pre-diabetic, meaning that while they don't yet have the disease, if they continue with their current lifestyles, they will almost definitely develop diabetes.

While there are some terrific medications on the market for controlling diabetes, blood pressure, cholesterol, and many other health-related issues, I believe, as do many health practitioners, that prevention is preferable to treatment, although I am sure that most pharmacists would disagree! Everybody knows that a good balanced diet and solid exercise routine are conducive to good health, yet comparatively few people actually take the required steps. I have listed some of the reasons for this below.

- Healthy food is too expensive.
- Gym membership is too expensive.
- I don't have the time.

- I'll start eating better/exercising tomorrow
- Nothing bad will happen to me.
- I'm fine the way I am.

Do any of the excuses above sound familiar? Unfortunately, there is no one silver bullet to ensure optimal mental physical and mental health, but there are some simple and hugely powerful tools at your disposal, one of which is fasting, which does not cost you any money, in fact it will save you money and time which you would have spent buying, preparing and eating food, you can also do it right now.

WHAT HAPPENS IN THE BODY DURING A FAST?

When you cut off your food supply, the body no longer has its usual source of glucose, the simplest form of sugar, needed for the process of respiration which produces energy to power your body. The body is then forced to trigger a process called gluconeogenesis, which enables the body to produce its own sugar. As it is now in conservation mode, your resting metabolic rate (the amount of energy the body burns at rest) becomes more efficient, which in turn lowers blood pressure and heart rate. Further into the fast, another process is activated, that of ketosis where the body switches from glucose to fat as its primary energy source, which is ideal for promoting weight loss via fat burning.

Physiologically speaking, fasting is a mildly stressful process, which in effect toughens up the body's cells, this happens thanks to a cellular mechanism known as autophagy. I like to think of autophagy as similar to putting in a new kitchen. No matter your skill or knowledge level of DIY, you will be aware that in order to install a brand-new kitchen, you must first remove the old one, autophagy is the same idea. The word literally means "self-eating" and what happens is cleaning mechanisms remove old or damaged components of cells throughout the body, while at the same time, growth hormone is upregulated to promote the production of brand-new components, effectively repairing and rebuilding the cells!

Types of fasting

1. **Time restricted fasting.**

    This is simply where you pick a window in the day where you allow yourself to eat. In today's society we tend to eat more out of habit rather than for necessity, which means that your body is always working to digest food, most of the time it is not even good wholesome food, but high sugar, low fat, low protein junk food. A major problem with consuming many small high sugar meals is that it causes your blood sugar levels to spike, which results in the body having to release insulin to bring the sugar level back under control, over time this can cause the body to become less sensitive to the effect of insulin, resulting in lifestyle-induced type 2 diabetes.

    If you restrict when you eat to a defined period of time, you give your body a chance to process what it has already consumed, and you prevent the constant blood sugar level fluctuations throughout the day. You can choose the duration and timing of your eating window, it can range from 6 to 12 hours, the shorter the window, the more you benefit. For example, you could choose to eat between the hours of 11am to 7pm, that way you can have a normal lunch, dinner and snack in-between, if you go to bed at

11pm and wake up at 7am, that is 8 hours completed out of your 16 hour fast! A further great benefit of abstaining from food and sugary drinks for several hours before bed is significantly improved sleep quality.

2. **Intermittent fasting.**

This type of fasting is simply where you fast every other day, for the whole day. Twenty-four hours to eat as much as you want, followed by twenty-four hours of strict fasting. There are arguments for reducing caloric intake to zero on fasting days, or simply reducing caloric intake to a significantly lower level, ranging from 60-100% but there does not appear to be a significant difference in fat loss between both approaches.

How fasting may help you

- **Enhanced fat loss and be extension, weight loss.**

  There are many studies proving the benefits of fasting on weight loss, one such study found an average weight loss of 5.2kg over a 12-week period of alternate day fasting for 49 men and women aged between 35 to 65 years old. Another study found that after 12 weeks, those who reduced their caloric intake by 75% for 2 non-consecutive days per week for a period of 12 weeks saw an average of 7.1kg of weight loss.

- **Enhanced mental clarity and toughness**

  Back in our hunter-gatherer days, we may have been forced to go days or even weeks without food, therefore our bodies had to adapt to these harsh conditions to keep us alive. When in a fasted state, as mentioned earlier, the body switches from burning glucose for energy, to burning fat, this switch is also accompanied by changes in the brain's neural networks which boosts the body's resistance to stress, injury, and disease.

- **Reduce inflammation throughout the body and lowered risk of disease.**

    So many diseases today are related to inflammation within the body, including diabetes, arthritis, irritable bowel disease, asthma, coeliac disease and many more. Fasting has been repeatedly found to lower the number of inflammatory proteins in the blood and in the brain, which may help in reducing the chances of developing these diseases and even possibly help ease the symptoms if they have already manifested.

- **Increased lifespan**

    There are five mechanisms by which it is thought that fasting may extend lifespans, some of which we have already addressed. Calorie restriction and intermittent fasting have been found to promote more controlled and efficient cell division, reduced inflammation throughout the body, increased energy production by the power plants of the cells, known as mitochondria, optimised repair and renewal of cells or autophagy and the production of antioxidants which help fight damage within the body as a natural part of aging.

- **Boosted confidence**

    As mentioned earlier in this chapter, this benefit arises from you stepping out of your comfort zone and into the unknown. The unknown is where great things happen in life because you are no longer on autopilot, making the same hard-wired, unconscious decisions. Just like in the ten dollar dare stories I previously outlined, when you consciously step out of your comfort zone and face new challenges, your body and mind adapt on a physiological level, and a side-effect of this is enhanced confidence, to meet and overcome the new challenge presented before you.

- **Elevated sense of self-esteem.**
   This benefit is likely a secondary result of the other benefits, or a positive feedback loop. You will feel a sense of achievement when you complete a fast, no matter the duration, and the more you do it, the more the results will compound over time, much like adhering to a solid gym training routine.

   My own personal fasting record is forty-eight hours, which I will admit was one of the toughest things I have ever done. I have completed dozens of smaller fasts ranging from sixteen to forty-eight hours, and for me, I feel that I get most benefit by limiting each stint to twenty-four hours. This is enough time to give my body a break from digesting the food within my system, while simultaneously giving me a boost in mental alertness and mood. When I was younger, I would get "hangry" if I went more than a few hours without eating, and even today when fasting, I can feel the familiar hunger prangs begin to surface after about twelve hours in, and this is where self-control, awareness of emotions and determination comes into play, because this huger will pass, if you persevere. When I finally cross the finish line of my self-imposed marathon, I feel as if I have won a battle against myself, which only encourages me to do it again in the near future., creating that same positive-feedback loop mentioned earlier.

As you have seen above, there are many potential benefits to be gained from making small changes to your eating patterns, but if you do decide to try a fasting routine, I recommend that you start off small, such as an eight hour fast, then gradually increase the duration to ten, twelve, sixteen hours etc. I also recommend that consult your physician before doing so, as I am not providing medical advice, but rather sharing some of the currently available peer-reviewed research in addition to my own personal experience. This is without doubt a fantastic tool in your arsenal of growth and self-improvement, one which costs no money, saves you time and has the potential to boost not only your physical health, but mental health as well, fast!

Chapter Five

FREE YOURSELF AND YOUR POTENTIAL BY BREAKING THE BONDS OF ADDICTION

"I have absolutely no pleasure in the stimulants in which I sometimes so madly indulge. It has not been in the pursuit of pleasure that I have periled life and reputation and reason. It has been the desperate attempt to escape from torturing memories, from a sense of insupportable loneliness and a dread of some strange impending doom."

– Edgar Allan Poe

We have previously looked at the importance of commitment and self-discipline when it comes to starting the day off on a positive note, boosting both your mental and physical health and enhancing your quality of life. In this chapter we are going to look at the phenomenon of habits and addictions, how they change the brain on a physiological level, how they can impact your life for better or worse and actionable steps that you can take to not only help you break bad habits and addictions, but how to replace them with better more constructive ones, which will complement your resolve to lead the best life you can live, helping you to realise your true nature, that is feeling great.

Habit vs addiction

As human beings, we are creatures of habit, we crave routine, because it is the familiar known, therefore it is safe. There is nothing inherently wrong with this, and it is not for me or anyone else to tell you that your routines or habits are necessarily bad, they could be great! First let's make some distinctions between a habit and addiction.

A habit is an association that you have established between a stimulus and a response, or in other words it is a conscious or subconscious behavioural reaction to something. For example, when you walk into the kitchen in the morning, you might turn on the TV to catch the morning news, if you do that every day, you might consider that a habit, which has become part of your morning routine. Other habits include constantly checking your phone, avoiding eye contact, biting your nails, playing with your hair, having late night snacks and cracking your joints, to list only a few.

An addiction on the other hand is more complex than a habit, and more often than not, can be much more insidious. Potentially, any behaviour or activity can become an addiction if it is used consistently to numb emotions such as trauma, grief, depression etc, which explains why alcohol, certain drugs and gambling are some of the most common addictions and plagues of modern society. They are developed over time and cause physical changes within the brain itself which we will drill into in more detail shortly.

Addictions and habits are similar in that they involve a cause-and-effect relationship, but this is where their similarities end. Unlike with habits, such as getting out of a certain side of your bed, addictions enslave the addict. The addict has virtually no conscious control over their urge to indulge their cravings, even when they know deep down that it is harmful to them, be it physically, socially, emotionally or financially.

It is important to make clear that certain habits and addictions can also be beneficial to you, to others and your community. An example of a good habit is putting the change you receive from a shop clerk into the charity box beside the till. This is obviously a good habit to have, as the money which you gave was given in the spirit of altruism, where you do good for the sake of doing good. The money you gave will go to help those less fortunate than yourself, which in turn will make you feel better about yourself, and this applies to all charitable acts of giving. An example of a constructive and beneficial addiction might be that like me you are addicted to buying self-help books or listening to self-improvement podcasts on a daily basis.

Do you have any harmful addictions?

- Is a particular behaviour directly or indirectly having a detrimental impact on your life?
- Do you find yourself hiding certain behaviours from friends or family for fear of them thinking less of you should they find out?
- Do you put yourself in risky situations time and time again to indulge a certain activity?
- When you stop partaking in a certain activity or behaviour do you experience withdrawal symptoms such as stress or anxiety?

If you answered yes to any of the above questions, then it is likely that you have some form of harmful addiction, but rather than ignoring it and looking in the other direction, the first step to liberating yourself from the shackles of any addiction is acknowledging that it is there, and accepting that it is there, at this current moment in time. I say at this current moment in time because nothing is written in stone. We live in an ocean of motion, change is all around us, from the changing of the seasons to the evolution of species, to the highs and lows of the stock market. Nothing stays the same, and that applies to you, your thoughts and your personality. If you have a **desire** to change something about yourself, coupled with a **plan** to do it and the **commitment** to see it through, you cannot and will not fail, but it takes those three components, fused together to form a trinity of power.

The exercise below is going to provide you with an opportunity to pause, reflect and take stock on the habits in your life. Do not be afraid to search deep within your mind, because the more honest you are with yourself, the more you have to gain from doing this powerful exercise.

Exercise 1a – List 5 good habits you have right now

1. _____

2. _____

3. _____

4. _____

5. _____

Exercise 1b – List 5 bad habits you have right now

1. _____
2. _____
3. _____
4. _____
5. _____

Exercise 1c – List any good addictions that you consider yourself to have right now

1. _____
2. _____
3. _____
4. _____
5. _____

Exercise 1d – List any bad addictions that you consider yourself to have right now

1. _____
2. _____
3. _____
4. _____
5. _____

Addictions can be serious, even life-threatening, which is why they should not be ignored until it is too late. If you feel that you need help, then get it, be it from your physician, friends, family, a support group, councillor, or even books, podcasts, etc. Living with an addiction is like living in a car, trapped on a roundabout, where all you do is go round in circles, never moving forward, robing you off your vitality and zest for life. Like with taking the car off the roundabout, you have to become aware of the fact that you are currently trapped in this Groundhog Day-like loop, and make the conscious decision to exit the roundabout, break the cycle and move forward with your life, all of which is very possible for you to do, if you desire it.

In chapter eight we are going to look at the various levels of consciousness, or emotional states and how it is fully within your power to choose which state you spend most of your time in. Two of the lowest frequency and most destructive states are guilt and shame, and it is these emotions you experience most intensely after giving into temptation and indulging a destructive addiction. It is impossible to feel good about yourself if you are trapped in an endless loop of addiction, where every time you give in, you fall down into a pit of despair. If you can successfully break the chains of an addiction that are keeping you in a low-vibe state, you will naturally rise up through the emotional spectrum to states of higher frequency, such as love, joy and peace, all you have to do is let go of any and all destructive behaviours, which I know can be easier said than done sometimes, but I can guarantee you it is worth the effort.

When somebody embarks on the journey of giving up an addiction, they are said to be in the process of "rebooting", which is a popular way of saying "reset to factory settings". There have been many reports of people claiming that abstention alone has cured them of their anxiety, depression, mood-disorders etc, but do not take this as medical advice, I am not advising you to substitute medical treatment or therapy with simply going cold-turkey, but what I am saying is that self-reflecting, becoming aware of any harmful addictions and addressing them can be a supremely powerful tool for you to add to your belt of "life-hacks" on your journey of self-improvement.

Addictions change the brain

When a drug addict injects a shot of heroin, or an alcoholic downs a pint of beer, or a middle-aged man indulges himself on a gentleman's website, the same thing is happening in all of their brains, in that they are stimulating their neural reward pathways. It takes about 21 days to make a habit, and 90 days to make a lifestyle change, likewise in the case of an addiction, the longer you indulge it, the deeper it takes root in the brain. Every time the reward pathway is stimulated, a switch-regulatory protein is deposited along those specific neurons called delta-fos-B, which for all intents and purposes can be thought of as breadcrumbs like in the Hansel and Gretel story. The breadcrumbs helped the children find their way back home, whereas in the brain, these neural breadcrumbs help you find your way down that very same reward response pathway.

The problem with the accumulation of this delta-fos-B is that it overtime it desensitises you to whatever stimulus it causes you to crave, which results in you having to find an ever bigger and more intense or novel stimulus to provide you with the same rush or satisfaction, unfortunately you will never achieve the same level of bliss or satisfaction that you did the very first time. This is why drug addicts tend to progress from lighter, gateway drugs to more intense and dangerous alternatives overtime. As with online pornography, substantial numbers of people find themselves craving ever-increasingly novel, erotic or unusual scenarios or activities. It's this insatiable desire for novelty which drives every addiction known to mankind today. The good news is that all of these changes are reversible, to a very large extent.

Every one of us has strengths and weaknesses, you included. You may know a lot about yourself, but likewise, there are likely many things that you do not know about yourself, it is these unknowns which can sometimes lead to problems. These unknown qualities can contribute to what is known as self-awareness deficiency syndrome, or SADS and can be something as harmless as talking with your mouth full of food, or it can be something more serious such as losing your temper when somebody says something which strikes a nerve with you and you retort, almost like a knee-jerk reaction.

You may be able to resist urges for hours, days or even weeks, but if you are solely trying to resist temptation by willpower alone, then you will more than likely relapse. There are many tips and tricks that you can utilise to help you along the way, which I will outline shortly, but before you try and eliminate destructive habits or addictions from your life, there are two things that you must do first.

Beating addiction

1. **Acknowledge that the addiction is there.** If you bury your head in the sand, the program that is your addiction will continue to operate within your mind, influencing all of your thoughts, emotions and actions. When you shine the

light of your consciousness upon the addiction, its hold over you lessens significantly.
2. **Accept that it is there.** Acceptance of what is, dissolves all resistance. When you remove resistance, that enables flow, and when you can step into a state of flow, you prime yourself for change.

Once you have taken the two steps outlined above, you are ready to start utilising the tools listed below to help you cut any addiction you might have out of your life, enabling you to raise your vibration and prime yourself for change, which will allow you to move towards the live the life that you want to live, and on your own terms.

- **Replace the old destructive behaviour with a new constructive one.** Picture a bucket filled with muddy brown water. What happens if you use a hose to add clean, clear water into the bucket? The dirty water is eventually displaced by the clean water, leaving behind only a bucket of crystal-clear water.
- **Take steps to avoid triggers for your addiction.** For example, if you suffer from addiction to online gambling or pornography, then do not take your phone into the bedroom, especially when you are going to sleep, mainly because this is the most likely setting for you to give in to temptation.
- **Find an accountability partner**, someone who you trust with your secret, and who you can count on for support when things feel tough. By scheduling accountability sessions with this person, you force yourself to commit to your cause. You and your partner decide how frequently you want or need check-in sessions, it could simply be a text, email or call once a day, or perhaps once every week or fortnight.

- **Reward yourself for big and small achievements.** If for example you set a period of time that you want to go without giving into whatever your temptation might be, once you hit your goal, reward yourself with a treat of your choice, as long as it isn't the thing you were avoiding in the first place!
- **Forgive yourself if and when you relapse.** You will more than likely relapse at some point along your journey, but that is all part of the process. Rome was not built in a day, likewise, unlearning old habits and breaking away from addiction are not a straightforward linear process. The main thing to remember here is to not beat yourself up if you fall off the wagon, as that will bring you all the way down into the low vibe territory of the emotional spectrum. Rather, accept that you slipped up, do not dwell on it, then simply carry on from where you left off. If you can do that, then you are one giant step closer to achieving victory over yourself.

"I'm not telling you it is going to be easy, I'm telling you it's going to be worth it."-

Art Williams

Chapter Six

YOUR BRAIN IS LIKE PLAYDOUGH, FOR YOU TO MANIPULATE

Who are you?

Have you ever thought about this question? Maybe you have, maybe you haven't, but it is a question that can elude people for the entirety of their lives. All too often people let themselves be defined by what other people tell them, such as their parents or their closest friends, or perhaps they might define themselves by the things they have done, the job they have, or perhaps by the religion they have always practiced with unwavering rigidity. The question of who you are is not one that can be answered by anybody other than you, but it is of my opinion that it need not be as complicated as you might have originally believed.

The skull is the home of the brain, and the brain is the home of the mind, but would you believe it if I suggested that you are not your mind? I first came across this concept in Eckhart Tolle's masterpiece, the Power of Now, and would recommend it to anyone seeking the path towards spiritual development. My view of the brain, mind and consciousness is the following. The brain is akin to the hardware of a computer, while the mind is the software. You are conscious awareness and are the operator of the computer which is your mind, with full access and control over the computer.

Your thoughts are like tabs in an internet browser. The more tabs you have open in a window, the more cluttered the window becomes and the less likely you are to return to actually read them, all the while reducing efficiency in your work as your attention is being split between so many different pages. Likewise, with your brain, the more thoughts you have swirling around your head, the less attention you can give each one, resulting in reduced efficiency in completing tasks, and also a substantial drop in quality in whichever tasks you are working on.

Arguably more importantly, the more thoughts you have bubbling in your mind, the more stress you are likely to experience. This is because you will inevitably be projecting into both the past and future, stepping out of the present moment, therefore siphoning energy out of the present moment which increases the likelihood of not finishing whatever tasks you had set out to complete in the first place, which in turn generates feelings of frustration, anger, guilt etc. In chapters seven and nine we will be focusing on what you can actually do to combat this, and much more, but for the moment we will be focusing on the brain itself.

The human brain is an enormously complex organ, with as many neurons (nerve cells) as there are stars in the Milky Way galaxy, which communicate via trillions of connections called synapses. These synapses are a literal electrical highway, transmitting signals throughout the brain, eyes and body via the optic nerves and spinal cord respectively at a staggering 268mph. To put it in real world perspective, that is as fast a Bugatti Veyron Super Sport hurtling down the German Autobahn at maximum speed! We know that sixty percent of the brain's composition is fat and that it isn't fully formed until the age of 25 years old. We also know that when the body is at rest, approximately one third of all calories being burned are being burned by the brain's metabolic activity. Thirdly, we know that the typical human brain can generate 23 watts of power, enough to literally power a light bulb!

I have only listed some of the amazing things which we know about our own brains, but let's now shine some light on the things we don't yet fully understand. We don't yet fully understand how information is actually coded within the neural activity of the brain, nor do we fully know how memories are stored and retrieved. How do we simulate the future in our minds? Why do our brains need sleep? What is intelligence? And possibly my favourite, what is consciousness? These are all tremendously profound questions, and we cannot hope to do them justice within a single book, but we will explore some of the most exciting aspects of the brain and how they can be harnessed and used to your advantage.

Neuroplasticity – your brain is malleable, like play dough

> *"Among other things, neuroplasticity means that emotions such as happiness and compassion can be cultivated in much the same way that a person can learn through repetition to play golf and basketball or master a musical instrument, and that such practice changes the activity and physical aspects of specific brain areas."*
> – Andrew Weil

Do you believe that people can change? Or are you of the belief that people's views and personalities are relatively fixed? I remember one time when I was visiting my dad at home, we were enjoying some Nespresso cappuccinos while watching the six nations rugby on TV, we were supporting the Irish team, as those in Northern Ireland tend to do, I can't remember how the game ended, but I suspect not well, as that season was altogether quite a forgettable one. I do however remember asking my dad during the half-time break the question, "Do you think that people ever change?"

My dad and I have always had many random and varied conversations over the years, so as random as this question may seem, it was not out of the ordinary by our standards at all. After hearing my question, he took some time to contemplate it, and I could see his mind at work as he mulled over my question. Eventually he replied with, "No, I don't think they do". We did not pursue this topic much further as the second half of the match was about to kick-off, and our team desperately needed our undivided attention and support.

Regarding the question I posed to my dad, his answer both surprised me and deflated me. This is a man who has met many people in his life, both successful and modest, from many different walks of life, and to hear this answer to my question was quite discouraging to me at the time, as I was in the early steps of my journey towards self-improvement. I was worried that he might be right, as from my own experience at that point, I admit that I had observed similar trends. People tended to do the same things, day after day, indulge in the same behaviours, talk about the same things etc. This is not necessarily a bad thing, for by nature we are creatures of habit, it only really becomes a problem if these patterns start damaging our health or welfare, or that of others.

Now however, after several more years of observation, study and experience under my belt, I can say with complete certainty, that people can and do change, for better or worse and it can either be by conscious choice, or by circumstance, such as a traumatic event, or some other form of wake-up call, for use of a better term. I have come to realise this through my own study of books, scientific literature, podcast interviews and simply by paying more attention to the people in my life and how they conduct their own lives.

In chapter eight we will focus on consciousness and the various emotional levels or states of consciousness, because having a map of the emotions will help you to determine where you are at right now and where you want to go. The lowest frequency emotions such as grief and despair are destructive, while the higher frequency states such as love, joy and peace are all constructive states. There are many different states in between, and all of us will move back and forward throughout a range of them in our lives on a daily basis, but there will likely be one particular emotional state that each person inhabits most of the time. On average though, over a lifetime, a person will most likely ascend by just one level, according to research performed by Dr Hawkins and discussed in his book Power versus Force, but it is possible to climb many levels up the emotional spectrum, or scale of consciousness, which we will address shortly.

Not only is it possible to upgrade your level of consciousness, but it is also possible to upgrade your brain by changing its wiring, this is made possible by an inbuilt mechanism all humans possess, known as neuroplasticity. Think of neuroplasticity as the neural equivalent of muscle building, but within the brain, the more often you do something, the better you become at it, and what you don't use, fades away. If you have ever crammed for an exam, you might have found that you remembered what you needed to, to get you over the line the next day, but how much of what you studied did you remember several days or weeks later? Probably not that much I'd wager, as you haven't created a reinforced neural pathway for that exam material, which can only be achieved through repetition. Each and every time you think a new thought, you create a new neural pathway, and each time you come back to that thought, its neural footprint becomes deeper and more entrenched, meaning that it will take longer to fade.

Neuroplasticity is facilitated by the process of neurogenesis, which means the growth and development of nervous tissue, or brain tissue and is an incredible process, as it literally creates new neurons and new connections between neurons throughout the brain. The more of these you have, the more effectively and efficiently your brain works! It was traditionally thought that neurogenesis only occurred in the developing nervous system during gestation, but since the turn of the century, this has been thoroughly disproven. Neurogenesis and therefore by extension neuroplasticity continue throughout the entire life of each and every human, although both processes do reduce with age over time, they never halt.

Brainwaves

The ease of which you can reprogram your thinking patterns and your belief systems correlates strongly with your predominant brainwaves and how you utilise them, which we will explore right now. We have previously addressed the existence of neurons and synapses within the brain (neural cells and connections between these cells, respectively). Brainwaves are synchronised pulses of electricity, which radiate across clusters of neurons communicating with each other and can be detected, measured, and quantified by placing sensors on the scalp and connecting them to what is known as an electroencephalogram, or EEG. First discovered in 1925 by German psychiatrist Hans Berger, while on a quest to discover and unravel the secrets of telepathy. Unfortunately for Berger, and all enthusiasts of such phenomena, no concrete evidence of telepathy has yet been found.

Think of brainwaves as different musical notes, constantly flowing throughout your brain ranging from low to high frequency, and they change depending on what you are doing, thinking, or feeling. They are divided into five main categories, delta, theta, alpha, beta, and gamma.

1. **Delta (0.5 to 3 Hz).** These are among the slowest of the brainwaves, which penetrate deeply into the brain. They are the predominant wave-type generated in deep dreamless sleep and deep meditation. Healing and regeneration of the mind and body occurs here, which is why good quality, uninterrupted sleep is so important for maintaining optimal health.

2. **Theta (3 to 8 Hz)**. Like delta, in that they are generated in sleep and deep meditation. Theta waves are regarded as being the portal to memory, intuition, and learning. This is the frequency level where vivid dreams occur, and intuition is at its peak. You experience this frequency at least two times every day, as soon as you waken in the morning, and as you are drifting off to sleep at night. It is during these two windows in the day that your brain are at its most susceptible to reprograming, and moulding your mindset, thoughts, and beliefs in whichever way you most desire. This is why it is crucial that you avoid your phone and any negative stimuli for the last hour and first hour of the day.

3. **Alpha (8 to 12 Hz)**. Think, flow-state. When things feel like they are going effortlessly for you, you are likely in a predominant alpha state. These waves are also present in light meditation and are associated with super-learning, calmness, alertness, and overall mental coordination.

4. **Beta (12 to 38 Hz)**. These are the main waves you experience while awake, when your attention is focused on cognitive tasks, such as driving, or when at work. In this frequency range, the sympathetic nervous system is more likely to be activated which can be an issue if you remain in this state for too long, as it consumes a tremendous amount of energy. These waves help with problem-solving, decision-making and judgement, but are also closely associated with both excitement and stress,

5. **Gamma (38 to 42 Hz)**. Think of these waves as the Ferrari of brainwaves. Fast, powerful, rare. Unlike beta waves, in gamma state rather than lose energy, you actually liberate and cultivate more energy within your body, you have risen beyond a survival state, and have reached a state of bliss. Brain coherence is at an all-time high, in that different regions communicate much more effectively with one another. In order to access this state, the mind must be quiet. Initially dismissed by neurology experts as "spare noise", until it was found to be active in highly charged emotional states, such as altruism and universal love. It is also thought that gamma waves play a role in modulating consciousness and perception.

This was a very brief introduction to brainwaves, and they are a fascinating subject in and of themselves, but all that I need you to appreciate right now is that they exist, how they are categorised and differ between one another, and how you can use them to aid you on your journey of growth and self-development. They will be mentioned again later in the book.

The Reticular Activating System – You see what you want to see

Have you ever set your heart on a particular car, something you maybe didn't pay much attention to before, perhaps it was something a bit different, like a full-size SUV to tow your brand-new twin-axle trailer, or an MPV to ferry your children and their three friends to and from football practice on Saturdays? You then start seeing this particular make, model or type of car appearing absolutely everywhere you look. You might have experienced this uncanny phenomenon in other areas of life, be it when looking for a partner, an item of clothing or maybe a song on the radio. This almost-matrix-like-effect is due to a particular feature hardwired into the neurology of the brain, known as the reticular activating system, or RAS for short.

The RAS is one of the most useful and powerful tools built into the hardware within your brain, as it literally lets you see whatever it is you seek. Think of it like a neurological, perceptual filter, which you have complete control over, if you so choose. Its main purpose is to protect you from sensory overload. At any given moment, there are up to one billion different stimuli all around you, and you can only take in a tiny proportion of this, somewhere in the vicinity of eight million bits of information, or approximately 0.8% of this, thanks to the RAS, and these bits of information go straight into your subconscious minds. What you actually see and perceive is dependent upon your thoughts, the story you tell yourself, your expectations and energy or consciousness level. When a message makes it past the RAS filter, it makes it into the brain's cerebrum, or thinking centre, where it is converted into conscious thoughts.

A personal example of this which I have seen in my life is my younger brother and his inability to find things in the house. When we all lived in the same home, many years ago, anytime that he was tasked with finding an item, it did not matter what it was, be it a book from the book shelf, the dog treats from utility room cupboard, or WD40 oil spray from the garage, the result would almost always be a defiant, "It's not there!" Now I love my brother, and I say this from a place of love and free from judgement, but he really was hopeless at finding anything back then, and we made that known to him. Years later after having learned of the existence of the RAS and how it is so closely linked to what we tell ourselves in the form of our personal beliefs and the story that we repeatedly tell ourselves, I realised that this particular trait of his was probably heavily influenced by myself and the rest of the family, creating the belief that he was not good at finding things, and then reinforcing that belief repeatedly over the years (If by chance you ever happen to read these words, I sincerely apologise James!).

Now the question is, how do you capitalise on all of this information to help you dissolve stress on a daily basis and enable you to take back control over yourself and your life, ultimately allowing you to unlock the natural feeling of greatness within?

Your thoughts, feelings and beliefs shape your reality

Most of your thoughts and feelings come from past experiences, which essentially means that the brain is largely a record keeper of all the things that you have learned and experienced to date. For every thought that you think, or event that you experience, the information relayed to your brain through the senses of sight, smell, hearing, taste and touch stimulates a jungle of neurons to organise into networks to string together the stimuli into patterns which reflect your interaction with the environment, at the same time, the brain also makes corresponding chemicals which create what we know as emotions. Each and every time you learn something new, or have a novel experience, that stimulates the brain to produce new neurons, which increases the degree of circuity organisation within the brain. In 2000, Nobel laureate Kandle found that learning just one new bit of information resulted in the brain creating up to 1300 new connections.

Unless you are one of the tiny minority of individuals who possess an eidetic or photographic memory, I assume that you have forgotten many things in your life, such as a wedding anniversary perhaps, or maybe you had agreed to collect a friend or family member from the city-centre bus stop, only to remember fifteen minutes after the time that you were supposed to meet them! On the other hand, you will no doubt have retained some very specific memories over a period of years or even decades, such as the feeling you had when you got your first car, graduated university, met your first love, etc. In short, what determines how well you remember an event or experience, is the amount of emotion you charge that particular thought with, be it a positive or negative emotion.

Thought is the language of the brain, and feelings or emotions are the language of the body. What you think and what you feel dictates your state of being, or in other words, the quality of your current experience. When you think and feel the same things over and over, this produces an attitude, which is a shortened state of being. When you repeatedly experience the same attitude, it eventually forms a belief. Beliefs are in essence the thoughts that you think repeatedly until they are hardwired into your brain, they are almost entirely based on past experiences and how you interpreted those experiences. By the age of thirty-five, about 95% of who you are is a set of habituations, or a collection of unconscious thoughts, actions, and behaviours.

Beliefs create subconscious states of being and when multiple beliefs are strung together, they determine how you perceive anything and everything that you come into contact with in this world, including but not limited to God, relationships, love, health, and spirituality. Now, since your perceptions are based on your beliefs, and if your beliefs are formed from past experiences, that means in actuality, you view life through the lens of the past, all unconsciously. You are seeing reality from past memory and overlapping the present moment with the colours of the past. You might wonder what the problem is with this, and I will address that question in the following chapter, but in a nutshell, I will be addressing the importance of staying present to the moment, because when you shift your attention from the present to either the past or the future, you siphon energy from the present moment, which in turn substantially reduces the number of possibilities which would have otherwise been available to you.

The good news is, as you may have already known, that you have complete power over what you believe and how you perceive things, and you can do it right now where you sit. In order to change any belief or perception, you must make a definitive decision, and charge it with such intention that the power of that decision carries a level of energy exceeding that of the hardwired programs in your mind and emotional conditioning of the body. If you can do this, you can override the current programs, and cause the body to respond to your new mind. When you change the internal experiences within your mind you reorganise the circuitry within the brain, which in turn sends all new emotional signals to the body, and it is from here, that you liberate yourself from the self-imposed chains of your past.

A fantastic real-world example of this is the classic story of a mother lifting a car off her child on the street. In that moment, she doesn't stop to think that she is not strong enough to do it, or that she hasn't been to the gym in however many months. What she does instead, is unconsciously shift her state of being to one of complete and utter certainty, that she must save her child. Once she makes this definite but albeit temporary change internally (in her mind) her body responds accordingly to this new mindset, and through the utilisation of the sympathetic nervous system, resulting in adrenaline charging through her body, her muscles contract at 100% capacity, enabling her to do what she would in normal situations deem to be completely impossible.

I hope that by this point you are starting to realise just how much power you have over your thoughts, your body and over your life. Through implementing some, or even better, all of the knowledge and tools that we have covered so far, you are well on your way to claiming back all of the power that you have lost through stress and the stories you tell yourself. When you claim back your power, you will discover your birth-right that is the pure, divine and natural bliss that is and always has been inside you, when you rediscover this bliss, you won't be able to feel any less than great, all the time. You are the writer of your story, the creator of your fate, nobody else.

Part 2 – Tools for the Mind and Soul

Chapter Seven

STAY IN THE NOW TO TRANSFORM YOUR LIFE

"All negativity is caused by an accumulation of psychological time and denial of the present. Unease, anxiety, tension, stress, worry – all forms of fear – are caused by too much future, and not enough presence. Guilt, regret, resentment, grievances, sadness, bitterness, and all forms of nonforgiveness are caused by too much past, and not enough presence."

- Eckhart Tolle

Over the course of my life, if I had a penny for every time my mum said to me "Your mind never stops!" I would have enough to buy a double-shot cappuccino with cream in any high street coffee shop. It was a lot because my mind really never did stop. When living at home throughout my time at school, and even when I returned home at 25 years of age to retrain as an optometrist at the University in the neighbouring town, just a stone's throw from my mum's home, I would constantly bombard my mum with political news that I had read that day, a particularly entertaining story that I may have heard in a podcast, or a new philosophical theory I had stumbled upon in a book, and more often than not, things that I declared that I wanted to do in the immediate and even distant future, such as starting a new website, learning a new instrument or climbing a mountain I hadn't yet scaled before.

As fun as it can be, having a racing mind which rarely stops, it can also be a curse, as it is very easy to go down the proverbial rabbit hole. Have you ever experienced something positive happen in your life, where you are filled with joy, only for that euphoria to subside in a matter of seconds, minutes, or even hours due to your mind over-analysing the event in your mind or creating hypothetical subsequent future events in your mind, which may or may not ever come to pass? I could literally think my way out of happiness in less than a minute.

A personal example of this in my life, (which I think a lot of people may be able to relate to) is when I was 17, I went on a date with girl that I was crazy about. She was smart, beautiful, very literate and had a similar taste in music to myself, which back then was a huge bonus for me, as I had just recently discovered the hidden gem of heavy metal, and was slightly obsessed with Metallica, Dragonforce and Disturbed, to name just a few. So strong was my infatuation with this girl that I committed to learning a new word every day, with the hope of impressing her with my evolving vocabulary, unfortunately the endeavour was not as salubrious for me as I would have hoped.

This was to be my first date, and needless to say I was nervous. My brother and I grew up in the Northern Irish countryside where we had a relatively isolated childhood, albeit a great one, nevertheless. I had no idea how as to how the perfect date should go, truthfully to this day I still feel somewhat clueless in this area, but when I was 17, I was like Bambi trying to walk on the ice, hapless. Eventually, date-day came, and it went great! Or at least I thought it went great. We went to Barry's Amusements in the coastal town of Portrush, which is to this day a brilliant day out for anyone.

After working our way through all of the rides and arcade games we drove round to the neighbouring village of Portstewart, where we went to the best ice-cream parlour in the country, Morelli's, which I would strongly recommend you visit if you ever find yourself in Northern Ireland, I especially recommend you try the Yellow Man! I will not bore you with any further details of the date, but suffice to say, it ended with me leaving her off home, where we hugged, hinted at the possibility of a second date, and said good bye. I was on top of the world!

Over the following days I created a completely imaginary relationship and future with this girl in my head, I suppose you could say that I had worn my heart on my sleeve. I thought I had found the "one" on my first date. Needless to say, this was not to be. As the days and weeks passed and the chances of a second date were all but extinguished, I had spiralled into a pit of despair. I allowed myself to project into a completely hypothetical yet vivid future and became so attached to it that it was almost impossible to let go. I was only 17, but it felt like my heart had been ripped out and my life was in tatters.

In hindsight, I am painfully aware of how much I blew things out of proportion, and that I was essentially trying to hold water in my hands. The only real saving grace was that almost all of this turmoil was merely in my own head and not sprawled across social media, nor did it involve any face-to-face hostility. I eventually did get over this would-be heartbreak, with enough time passing by to ease the wound.

This cycle would be repeated again only 5 years later, with another girl that I met one Halloween at the local rock bar, needless to say I got a little bit more than a hug this time, but I made the same mistake of mentally projecting into the future where I had the perfect relationship with the perfect girl and everything was, you guessed it, perfect. This was destined to result in another spell of misery when my imagined fantasy future did not come to fruition. These are but two examples in my life where living in the future has resulted in bitter disappointment, frustration, and sadness. You may have experienced something very similar yourself. It wasn't until several years later when I embarked upon my journey of self-improvement that I discovered the tools to make sure this never happened again.

A NATION CHAINED TO THE PAST

All stress, misery and frustration in life comes from stepping outside of the present moment. When you project in to the future or look back to the past, what you are essentially saying to yourself is that the present moment is not good enough, but if you pause and reflect on what the present moment is, you will come to realise that it is all you have, all you have ever had, all you ever will have. The all-time classic Power of Now by spiritual teacher Eckhart Tolle is dedicated to this concept and really drills down into what it means to be present to the now, how it will benefit you and how you can tap into it. I understand how esoteric this may sound at first, but when you pause and truly reflect on it objectively, you will come to see the truth. I am not saying that it is bad to look to the future, or reminisce of good times in the past, it only becomes a problem when you are constantly projecting, and rarely staying present in the moment.

Let me give you a large-scale example of what happens when you continually live in the past. My home country of Northern

Ireland has had a troubled past, as have many countries. There was a period known as the Troubles which lasted from 1968 to 1999. I will not go into detail of the conflict as that is not within the scope of this book, but in essence what happened was the two largest communities in the country were at war with one another. Lives were lost, homes and businesses destroyed, it was a very dark time in our history. Peace was finally brokered in 1999 in the form of the Good Friday Agreement, while it did not solve all of the problems, but it did effectively end the war through a power-sharing agreement, and for the first time in three decades, Northern Ireland had peace.

Many people have successfully moved on, but there are many who have not, and it manifests in their lives, neighbourhoods and beyond. They choose to hold on to ills against them and their families, committed all those years ago, they may be seeking justice through the courts, or they may simply still carry a grudge against members of the other community. Whatever the reason for their holding onto the past, one thing is for certain, is that it does not serve their mental wellbeing, holding onto the past, because it siphons energy away from the here and now, and they cannot experience change, growth and joy when living in the past, that can only be found in the present moment.

You will no doubt be able to think of countless examples where you have seen or experienced this first hand, countries, people, or even yourself, dwelling on a past wrong, or imagined future scenario which may or may never come to fruition. This does not serve you. If you want to truly liberate yourself from this psychological baggage, simply let go and draw your attention to this very moment. A fantastic phrase I came across years ago is, "Where thought goes, energy flows". If you bang your shin against the coffee table as you are scrambling up to refill your mug with your favourite caffeinated beverage, the chances are that you will produce a string of choice profanities. You rub your shin and eventually the eye-watering pain will subside. Now think about this, when you bang your shin against the table, you have one choice with two options.

You can choose to focus on the pain, and let it run its course, or you can choose to ignore the pain and be present in your surroundings, focusing on everything else, being present in the moment. This may sound confusing, but in essence what it means is, if you focus on your shin, you will feel more pain, if you take your focus off your shin and place it on for example, staying present, or something entirely different, like the clock hanging on the wall, you will find that both the intensity and the duration of the pain is substantially diminished.

Where thought goes, energy flows

You will see the above statement above numerous times throughout this book, because it is such a critical rule to remember and always bear in mind. When you place your attention excessively on either the past and/or future, you are siphoning your creative energy out of the present moment, and if the first thing you do each and every morning when you wake up is reach for your phone, check your emails, browse the morning news, think about the tasks of the day ahead, the family schedules, grocery shopping to be done etc, your energy becomes fractured, it is like spreading an inadequate amount of butter over a large slice of toast.

For each person, place, task, or thing you give attention to, you do so because you have previously experienced it and therefore it occupies a specific neurological network within your brain, this applies to all things in your life. The more attention you give to that thing, the more consolidated that neural network becomes, almost like a neurological footprint within the brain. This is why the more novel experiences you expose yourself to, the more neural adaptation and rewiring occurs, enriching the brain. When you spend all of your energy focusing on these external entities, the less energy you have left over for yourself to create something new within. This is important because your inner reality determines your outer reality, and if you do not have adequate energy to tend the garden of your inner-self, or thoughts, then your outer reality will be completely out of your control and almost-completely subject to external influence rather than your own inner influence.

How you think and how you feel is what determines your reality, so you need be constantly aware of what thoughts are entering and taking up residence in your mind and where you are allocating your mental energy. It is for these reasons that the vast majority of people rarely change throughout their lives because they are thinking the same thoughts, feeling the same feelings, and doing the same motions. To quote Tony Robbins, "If you do what you've always done, you'll get what you've always got". When you realise that your feelings are determined by what you think, and that most of your thoughts arise from a dwelling on a familiar past or predictable future, you have taken a massive step towards unearthing your inner happiness, which will enable you to feel great, almost all of the time.

Furthermore, what you think and what you feel broadcast an electromagnetic signature, which I will elaborate on later in this book. If you are constantly focusing on the knowns in your life, where you are living in a familiar past and predictable future, you broadcast the exact same signal at all times, and it is very likely that your life will never change, certainly never for the better, for you are simply re-creating the past, over and over and over again. If you stay trapped in this never-ending loop, you will be not too far removed from Bill Murray in his 1993 classic, Groundhog Day, except less hilarious.

To escape this endless feedback loop, you have to break the cycle, to break the cycle you have to pause when reaching for your phone first thing in the morning. Pause when you start projecting excessively into the day ahead, and instead take time to find the moment and focus on the here and now, a great way to do this is to have a cold shower, which forces you into the present moment, shutting off the incessant stream of thought!

A barrel of fun

After graduating from university with my degree in optometry I had some time to relax and recuperate from the intense previous academic year. I remember sitting at my desk in my dad's house, seeking inspiration for a new project that I could sink my teeth into, ideally one that could generate some money too. It was almost as if fate itself intervened directly, because as I was killing some time by scrolling through my Facebook newsfeed (something which I very seldomly do now) when I noticed an ad for a local Whiskey distillery, with some casks in the background, my brother happened to be in the room at the same time (he is quite the whiskey enthusiast and a great idea generator) and I asked him could anything be done with a whiskey cask, to which he immediately replied "They can be converted into a cabinet".

I immediately did a Google search for whiskey cabinets and

was blown away by what people had done. Other people before me had taken old, weathered, and rusted casks and converted them into chic things of beauty which would not look out of place in a cosmopolitan penthouse! I was convinced as to how I would spend the next week, making my own whiskey cask cabinet.

It did not take long to source some old casks and before the end of the day I had acquired two brand new… I mean, old casks. I had managed to find an instruction tutorial to help me with my latest mission, after watching it several times, I was ready to take on my first cask. Over the years I had gained a degree of experience in DIY and how to do the basics, such as sawing, sanding, painting, changing wall plug sockets etc, but it did not take me long to realise that I had my work cut out for me with this one. Fortunately, I had the whole house and garage to myself, most of the time, as my dad and step-mum were away on holiday, and my brother was working at his job throughout the day. I will not go into every detail of each step along the process, but I will share what I found throughout the process.

The first step, and in hindsight, the single biggest step was to sand the entire cask, from top to bottom, which turned out to be a real test of grit by itself! My dad has a great collection of tools, so I made use of his electric hand-held sander, which worked fantastically. It took more hours than I can count to sand the whole thing. Sanding any longer than fifteen to twenty resulted in mild hand spasms at the start, but after some time, my hands seemed to adapt, thankfully. It did not take long before I lost myself in the process, I entered a flow state, each and every time I started work on the cask. Time seemed to fly by, and before I knew it, I could have spent many consecutive hours sanding every square inch, starting with course grit sandpaper to remove the outer roughness, before progressing to fine grit to achieve a flawless, glass-like smooth finish.

The project forced me to don my thinking cap and flex my problem-solving muscles numerous times, such as figuring out how to hold the barrel staves (which would form the doors) in place while the glue binding them was setting. I also had to commission a local carpenter to create an appropriately sized shelf to insert into the body of the cask. For what appeared to be a relatively simple project at first, ultimately ended up being a real challenge, but one that I was happy to endure, because in my mind I had committed 100% to realising my vision of creating my cabinet.

To me, this was a test of my commitment and creativity, as well as giving me a chance to play with some of my dad's tools. Looking back, I absolutely loved this project, it allowed me to focus all of my energy and attention into a single short-term goal, almost like a form of meditation, which forced me completely into the present moment. To paraphrase Eckhart Tolle, we do not gain joy through what we do, but rather, we gain joy through something that we are completely channelling all of our presence and consciousness into.

On a further note, I will say that the cabinet did in fact turn out quite well! It was not perfect, as it turned out that when adding the hinges to the doors, this made it difficult fitting the doors into the original opening, which resulted in me having to spend many more hours sanding the doors bit by bit to shave off just a couple of millimetres from each one, to enable them to just about slot into place. In the end I even managed to sell the cabinet for a small profit within a few short weeks, which was just the cherry on the cake as far as I was concerned.

Finally, if you have any desire to explore a new hobby or craft, I would completely and unequivocally say without reservation, just do it. Set some time aside for a few days, or longer and commit all of your energy to see what you can create. You will enter a flow-state when you find your rhythm, the time will seemingly melt past and you will lose yourself in the moment. By the time you are finished, you will feel a fantastic sense of calm and satisfaction, and even a yearning desire to go further and see what else you are capable of.

"The ability to be in the present moment is a major component of mental wellness." – Abraham Maslow

Chapter Eight

CONSCIOUSNESS, YOUR TICKET TO CLOUD NINE

"Control of consciousness determines the quality of life."
– Mihaly Csikszentmihalyi

The topic of consciousness is as vast as the oceans of planet earth, and then some, but here we will address some of the key concepts of consciousness, including what we believe it to be based on our current understandings, a map of the different levels of consciousness available to everyone of us, and finally, how you can begin to take control of your own consciousness and use it to change how you view yourself, allowing you to realise the natural states of love, joy and peace already residing within you.

What is consciousness?

Simply put, consciousness describes your individual awareness, which includes your thoughts, feelings, emotions, and sensations. It is what makes each and every one of us unique. In the early 20th century, renowned psychiatrist Sigmund Freud postulated the existence of three distinct levels comprising human consciousness: conscious, subconscious, and unconscious. Following the Freudian model, the conscious level occupies about 10% of the mind's total capacity, while the subconscious and unconscious comprise on average 55% and

35% respectively.

From our understanding, the conscious mind has two main functions; the ability to direct our focus in whatever direction we so choose, and to enable us to imagine things which are not real. The subconscious mind is comparable to the random-access memory (RAM) of a computer. It is the storage facility for any and all recent or long-term memories such as the name of a client you just met for the first-time last week, or your other half's mobile phone number. It also houses the software for programs that you use on a daily basis, such as recurring thoughts, habits, behavioural patterns, and feelings.

Have you at some time or another found yourself driving along a familiar route that you have driven many times before, such as the commute home from work? You are driving along as normal, and then you suddenly come to realise that you have no recollection of the previous eight miles! Don't worry, I will not judge you, because it is something that has happened to many of us at least once, and anyone who denies it is probably lying. The reason why this happens is quite simply, you are not present in the moment, you slip from the state of conscious awareness into an automatic subconscious routine, or autopilot. This is obviously not ideal when operating a heavy piece of machinery, so from this point out, I strongly recommend that you make a conscious decision to be present, every moment that you are behind the wheel of your car, thus keeping you and everyone around you that much safer.

Thirdly, we have the deepest level, that of the unconscious mind, this is where all of your oldest memories and experiences live. Consider it the basement of your mind, or better yet, an underground neuro-library containing any and all repressed trauma you may have experienced at any point in your life.

While buried under much psychological soil, these repressed memories and experiences can grow like unchecked weeds in a garden which can end-up influencing your conscious thoughts, attitudes, beliefs, and behaviours.

Conscious 10%

Subconscious 50-60%

Unconscious 30-40%

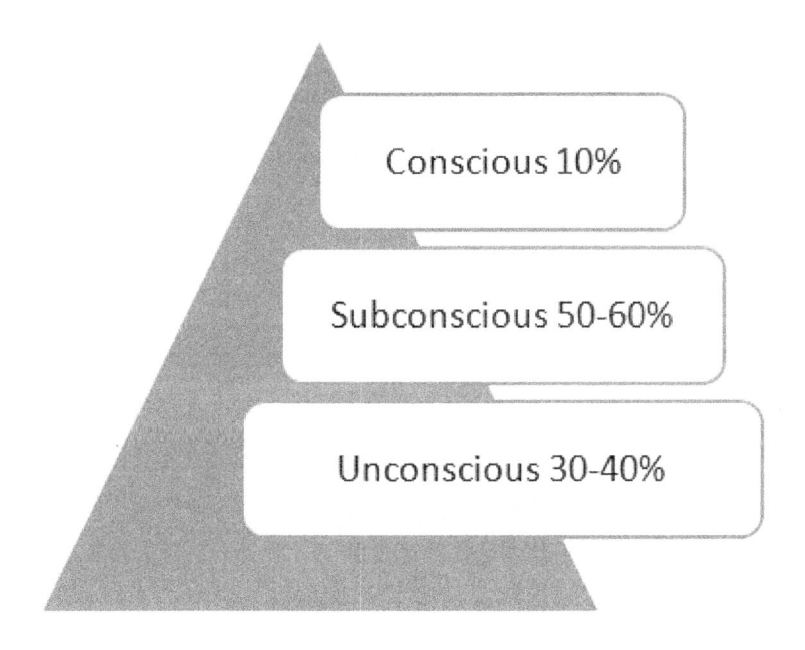

Figure 1. The three distinct levels of human consciousness as presented by Freud

The dimensions of our perceived reality

Through the advancement and development of our understanding of the universe and everything within it, we know of the existence of different dimensions. According to string theory, the universe operates within ten dimensions! In string-theory, the focal belief is that everything within the universe is comprised of infinitely small vibrating strings, permeating every atom of space. Consciousness, like the universe is comprised of different dimensions, or densities, known as 3D, 4D and 5D. You do not stay fixed in one dimension all the time, but you fluctuate between two or even three dimensions, depending on what is going on in your mind and in your life at that time. Despite the fact that we all inhabit the same planet, how we perceive things is determined by our state of consciousness

3D – A MATERIAL WORLD OF FEAR

In this state of consciousness, you view things from a purely physical perspective, and you perceive everybody as individuals, completely separate from everyone else. This is a life of absolutes, that there is only one life. It is possible to still accept the existence of a god, or higher entity, but you will feel completely distinct and separate from it. Here, life feels like it is survival of the fittest, and you identify strongly with how you look, the car you drive, the role you occupy in society and your social status. There is a constant fear of missing out, or not having enough material items or titles. Life is a competition, and things are binary, i.e., good, or bad. There are not enough resources to share with everyone, and fulfilment can only be achieved through making money and climbing the social ladder. Your thoughts have no power over your personal reality, and anything that comes your way is purely a result of happenstance and coincidence.

You may have noticed, but everything described in the preceding paragraph eerily describes the modern school system, with alarming accuracy, possibly explaining why the education system fails so many young people in not adequately preparing them for life and even more importantly, failing to teach them how to learn about themselves. From a young age we are all instilled with the fear that if we do not do well in tests, we cannot go to university, which means that we cannot acquire a good job worth having, resulting in a poor-quality life.

While not as easy and natural as it is in the higher realms on consciousness, it is still possible to obtain joy in living a 3D life, such as witnessing the birth of a child, watching a magnificent sunset, or perhaps being intimate with a partner. It is in these fleeting moments that we are firmly in the present moment, the now, the only place that the egoic mind cannot exist. The rest of the time, the ego is turbo-charging our monkey-minds to continually project into the past and/or the future, playing the dreaded "should have, would have, could have, what if game" and as you now know, the more often you step out of the now, the less happy you become, and the higher your stress and anxiety becomes, due to the fact that you are unconsciously telling yourself that the current moment is not good enough and are accumulating psychological time as a side-effect.

At this level, it can be difficult to handle pain and the deeper emotions of sadness, grief, despair etc. You believe that you can only find wholeness when you have a partner, that you rely on someone else to enable you to feel joy, this correlates with the study mentioned earlier in chapter 1, where 50% of volunteers could not bear to be alone with their thoughts, and opted to shock themselves, rather than be alone with themselves for just a short amount of time.

Moving back to the physical world, the reason why human beings crave sex so much is because at the 3D level it is the only chance, we get to experience something akin to pure joy, via the complete merging of both masculine and feminine energies, in perfect harmony. It is in fact possible to create this sense of completeness within ourselves and is actually a necessity if you intend to ascend to the next dimension of consciousness, 4D. To do this, you must learn to love yourself. Like me, you may have grown up believing that it is egotistical and narcissistic love yourself, but in reality, the opposite is true. Look at it this way, if you cannot love you, then how can you possibly expect somebody else to?

Within the 3D realm, you are a victim to the illusion of duality, where you experience light and darkness, things as good or bad, joy vs despair etc. Owing that we all have free-will to act and believe as we see fit, it is up to us how we perceive what we see, and how we respond to stimuli in our environment. But how often do you truly exercise this free will? Much of the time, we simply adapt to our surroundings and follow the crowd, because it is better to simply fit-in, than stand out. Thankfully, you are not locked into this level of consciousness.

4D – GATEWAY TO THE MAGICAL WORLD

This state is regarded as being the gateway to the fifth dimension, or 5D level. When in 4D, you may find that you can travel freely between 3D and even up to 5D. In this state, you begin to open up to the idea that we as humans are all connected, and that there is more to the world than what meets the eye. It is here that you start to realise and appreciate the power of your thoughts and the impact that they can exert over your personal reality. You have not yet risen above duality at this point, that is to say, you still experience and define most things as one or the other, good or bad, binary, in other words, although you are much more aware of this conventional way of viewing the world.

Many other changes begin to manifest at this level. You

may find that you begin reflecting on your current lifestyle, taking stock in what food you consume, how much alcohol you drink, the exercise you engage in. You may suddenly discover the appeal in and see the benefits of meditation and integrate it into your daily routine. Furthermore, there may be a shift in attention towards your impact on both your local environment and the people around you. A strong desire may arise within you to find and follow your purpose, or passion, because you have realised that life is meant to be enjoyed to the full, and that you are worthy to lead the life you desire.

5D – THE PLANE OF HIGHER CONSCIOUSNESS

Like with most things in life, once you experience the good stuff, it is hard to revert back to the lesser, lite version that you previously had grown accustomed to. You might even consider it as comparable to the red pill philosophy from the science-fiction Matrix trilogy. If you have not yet seen the Matrix, I strongly recommend it, not just for its ground-breaking at the time cinematic special effects or ultra-dynamic fight scenes, but for the philosophical undertones permeating the entire franchise.

In short, humanity has become enslaved by machine overlords and are living imprisoned within a virtual world known as the Matrix. The main character Neo is offered a choice by the leader of a band of resistance fighters, in the form of a red pill and a blue pill. If Neo chose the blue pill, he would remain in the Matrix, asleep, or blissfully oblivious to the fact that he is living in a simulated world. If he were to choose the red pill however, he would be freed from the virtual chains binding his mind and body, liberating him from the lie that was his entire world and allowing him to see things as they really were. I will not give any more spoilers just in case you have not yet seen this must-see movie!

At the 5D level of consciousness, you will be able to see through the veil of conventional wisdom and thinking encouraged and propagated in the modern world. At this point, you truly know that this world is not one of lack, but one of abundance. You will experience more frequent and extended bouts of overwhelming emotions of love, joy, peace and compassion for people, the earth, and the universe. You may feel like your intuition has reached a new level, everyone is equal in your eyes, and you have a strong and immutable desire to live from a place of complete authenticity. There will still be trying times in life, but they will not bring you down or sit on your mind the way they would have done when you inhabited a lower level of consciousness. This is because you have come to fully realise and accept that you are an eternal spiritual being, having a temporary human experience. Becoming aware of this truth will help enable you to manifest the life that you want, and almost everything will feel effortless.

Levels of consciousness

We humans are linear creatures, that is to say we think in terms of forward or backward, up, or down, more, or less. Examples include the passing of time, the acceleration of a car from 0-62 mph, the rising and falling of a thermometer, the examples are limitless and everywhere to see. We love thinking in terms of levels, or hierarchy, just look at the structure of any military, company, or government. Remaining true to this tradition, we can qualitatively rank all of the different emotional states of consciousness in order from most negative and destructive to most positive and constructive. Once you become aware of each individual level, coupled with mindfulness of where you are emotionally, you can begin to take conscious control of your emotional state, an invaluable tool to wield, especially in today's fast-paced, high-stress society.

Shame

The lowest emotional state of mind that a person can inhabit. Each of us have no doubt experienced this level at some point, so suffice to say, it is not a nice place to be. There are many ways that a person can end up down here such as from a childhood trauma, or from psychological manipulation to name only two, too much time in this state of mind will eventually result in physical manifestations in the form of chronic sickness, ailments and potentially even death.

Guilt

Rivalling shame as the most destructive of all the states of consciousness, guilt has undoubtedly plagued each and every one of us at some time or another. It can sprout from a small seed of grief or apathy when planted in the mind, be it by your own actions, or thoughts, or as a weapon used by someone else seeking to hurt you or gain leverage over you in the form of emotional blackmail. A powerful thought to consider is this, you are not punished for your sins, but rather you are punished by your sins, due to your own self-created shame. When you feel bad, you tend to attract more negativity into your life, likewise when you feel positive, you tend to attract more positive experiences into your life, which we will explore in more detail later on.

Fear

Perhaps you have heard the phrase "there is nothing to fear but fear itself", declared by Franklin Roosevelt at his 1933 Presidential election. There is much truth to this statement. Fear in small doses is beneficial for your survival, especially when in unfamiliar or hazardous environments as it keeps your senses on high alert but like with staying in a prolonged state of stress, living in constant fear is obviously no way to live. There are several main fears from which all fears originate from, they are the fear of old age, poor health, death, loss of love, poverty and criticism.

Take a moment to think of something that scares you now, can you see how it links to one or more of the aforementioned root fears? A great way to do this is the "and then what?" exercise. For example.

"I am scared of not doing my job well"

"And then what?"

"Then I might get criticised by my boss"

"And then what?"

"I might get fired"

"And then what?"

"I won't earn any money"

"And then what?"

"Then I won't be able to pay my bills or buy food"

"And then what?"

"I could end up homeless, where I might starve to death"

As you can see from the example above, the root fear is that of death. Death is an inevitability that every living organism in creation must encounter, so it does not make sense to waste time and energy worrying about something that is unavoidable. Naturally, you do not want it to come earlier than you would ideally prefer, and if you end up broke and homeless, then yes, there is arguably a greater chance of an untimely demise, but in order to even get to that point, as you can see above, there are many proceeding events which must take place first. When you take the time and effort to trace the origins of any fear that you have, you set yourself up to be in a position where you can significantly lessen its hold over you, simply by shining the light of your consciousness on it, accepting that it is there, before simply letting go of it. In small doses, fear can be an effective motivator, but as with many things in life, too much will cripple you.

The emotion of fear has long been used as a tool to exert control over groups of people. Religious leaders have used it, politicians have always used it, and now in the modern age, the media uses it relentlessly and unashamedly. When people are kept in a chronic state of fear, they are much more susceptible to influence, be it by the influence of an enemy, government or work colleague. A basic formula for exploitation through fear is simply target a group of people with a message that instils fear in their minds, then provide them with a solution that solves their problem, whether or not the problem was ever really there in the first place is irrelevant, because if the people believe it to be true, then it is true for them in their reality, and they will gladly pay for anything that will provide them with the safety and security they so crave.

An example of this is informing a group of people that their community's water supply is contaminated with a toxin that causes cancer, this will cause them to panic and beg for a solution to this problem, a company which produces water filters then targets this community, assuring them that by installing one of their filters, they will eliminate the risk of drinking contaminated water, preventing them from losing their health providing them all with peace of mind.

Excessive fear prevents you from stepping out of your comfort zone and growing as an individual. Like liberating an electron from an atom which requires energy, it takes energy to wilfully extricate yourself from your comfort zone, such as willing yourself to step into a cold shower or bath, but once you overcome that initial barrier, you will quickly realise that there really was nothing to fear but fear itself.

Desire

Many great business leaders, entrepreneurs, motivational speakers and life-coaches say that the path to achievement starts with desire, and they are right, because it is the vital first step of every journey, but that is all it is, the first step. Personally, I view desire as a springboard to the higher emotional levels of consciousness and should be used as a basis for your motivation to improve in whatever way you choose, be it improving your health, finances, skill in a particular craft or relationship goals etc. The danger of staying too long at this level is that it is the level of addiction, be it the craving for money, status, or attention. There will never be enough to satisfy, which is why for example, many millionaires never have enough money, and continue accumulating more and more, due to an insatiable desire. Another risk of staying at this level for too long is that a prolonged state of desire can lead to frustration, which arises from a sense of lacking that which you crave.

Courage

This is the pivotal point of consciousness, where everything above this point is constructive and results in personal growth and below this level is regressive and destructive. It is here where you can start to feel empowered in your life as you have risen above the limitations of the lower levels such as desire, guilt, and shame. If you spend the majority of your time below this level, you will likely see yourself as a victim of circumstance but rise above it and you take your power back over your life. At this level, you will find that you have the energy required to learn new skills, start a new job, or to take a leap of faith in some aspect of your life. When you reach the level of courage, if you have not already, you will really begin to see significant growth in all areas of your life.

Acceptance

It is at this level that a significant transformation in both mindset and worldview occurs. Here, you will come to realise several things; firstly, that you are the creator of your own experiences in life, that life does not happen to you, but rather it happens for you. Like taking your power back and relinquishing your victim status at the lower level of courage, you will build upon that change at this level. Another substantial development at this level of consciousness is that you come to realise, that happiness does not come from extrinsic sources, but instead, it comes from within. Everything else such as cars, jewellery, job status etc are all simply noise and distractions from your true inner essence. Once at this level, stress will no longer be a burden for you to bear, for you will be in a permanent state of calmness, which will allow you to see and interpret things without personal distortion and prejudice.

Love

This is the level of true happiness, and relatively few people ever truly reach this level, but that should not discourage you, because the fact that you are even reading this book, firmly sets you within a small subset of individuals committed to developing and improving themselves, physically, mentally and spiritually. The love experienced here is unconditional and permanent. It is a state of being which enables you to focus on the good in the world and all life held within, while dissolving the negative by recontextualising it and breaking down barriers between all people that you come into contact with.

Joy

Not to be confused with an acute burst of joy that you might experience such as when you experience some good fortune in life. Instead, this is a state of prolonged, or permanent joy, which accompanies you in many or all activities that you take part in, which can range from simply sitting in a meditative state, to driving your car along your favourite road with your favourite song playing on the stereo. I view this emotional state as one of pure bliss, and deep compassion, even more so than at the level of love just below. If you are predominantly in this state you will view the world as it really is, a place of breath-taking natural beauty, and you will always view things from a "glass is half-full" perspective. Everything will feel somewhat effortless, you will be in a semi-permanent flow-state and synchronicities will happen more and more often.

A famous example of someone reaching this level can be found in the classic story by Charles Dickens' a Christmas Carol. The story's main character Ebenezer Scrooge was a notorious miser in the city of London, who despised the poor, underpaid his employees and hated Christmas. Long story short, he was subjected to a traumatic event in the form of being visited by four ghosts, the first one being the ghost of his deceased former business associate Jacob Marley who warned him that if he did not change his ways then he would be condemned to the fiery depths of hell for all eternity. Marley's ghost also warned Scrooge that he would later be visited by three ghosts that night, the ghosts of Christmas past, present and future. If you have not read the story, I strongly recommend that you check it out.

After being shown the errors of his ways by the ghosts, this triggered a transformation deep within Scrooge, literally overnight. He let go of everything that he was before and allowed pure, unadulterated love and joy into his heart, filling him with the Christmas spirit, which he carried with him all year round, turning him from the most despised man in London, into one of the most beloved men in the city, known far and wid0e for his warmth, joy and compassion. I am not saying that you need to be visited by a series of ghosts to reach this level, but for many people, it takes a traumatic event to trigger this kind of transformation, but it can also be achieved another way, which I will now share with you.

HOW TO USE THE ABOVE KNOWLEDGE TO YOUR ADVANTAGE

"The real source of 'stress' is actually internal; it is not external, as people would like to believe. The readiness to react with fear, for instance, depends on how much fear is already present within to be triggered by a stimulus. The more fear we have on the inside, the more our perception of the world is changed to a fearful, guarded expectancy. To the

fearful person, the world is a terrifying place. To the angry person, the world is a chaos of frustration and vexation. To the guilty person, it is a world of temptation and sin, which they see everywhere. What we are holding inside colours our world. If we let go of guilt, we will see innocence; however, a guilt-ridden person will see only evil."

– Dr David Hawkins, from Letting go

As I have mentioned before, emotions, or states of consciousness at the bottom of the scale weigh you down. An example which you will likely be able to relate to is where you are in work and have had an argument with a colleague over a work-related issue, and you are in a state of anger. You have two options; hold onto the anger and allow it to taint every encounter you have with other colleagues and customers, preventing you from performing to the best of your ability and entering a flow-state, resulting in your number of sales or conversions dropping, meaning that you miss your targets for the day, which could end-up in you having to work harder the following day to make up for the sub-par previous day, which causes more stress in and of itself than the original argument did in the first place.

The other option you have available to you is to simply let go of the anger as soon as you walk away from your colleague, because it does not serve you. When you turn away from them, turn away from the anger you feel arising in you, and stay present to the now. If you stay present in the now, it is impossible for you to remain angry at your colleague, because that anger arose from an argument, which happened in the past, but you do not live in the past, you are in the present moment, right now.

A helpful analogy I like to think of when it comes to letting go of negative emotions weighing you down is to think of a typical Jungle movie where one of the stars gets stuck in quicksand, the more they struggle and fight against the sand, the further and quicker they sink. But, when they slow their struggles, lie back and relax, allowing their weight to spread out, they are able to extricate themselves from a potentially fatal situation. Perhaps a more relatable example is in your local swimming pool. Which is the easier way to simply float on the water's surface, continuously kicking both of your arms and legs, non-stop in a battle against fatigue, a battle you can never win, or simply lying back like in the quicksand scenario and letting your body do what it does naturally, and float to the surface? All you have to do is let go, and you will naturally and effortlessly rise up to a higher emotional frequency, to your natural state.

Your natural states are those of love, joy, peace and bliss, you have simply forgotten it. You have forgotten it because you have become identified with your mind and the environment of stressors around you. You are not your mind, your mind, as mentioned earlier is the computer, and you are the operator of the computer, or more accurately, you are the conscious awareness which has access to the mind. When you become identified with the mind, you can literally think your way out of happiness. The mind continually looks for problems, this is partly a survival mechanism which has remained since our hunter-gatherer days, it is also partly egoic, the voice inside your head which tells you that you are not good enough and that you don't deserve happiness.

Once you learn to become aware of your thoughts and emotions, and realise that they are not who you are, rather that you are simply an awareness temporarily experiencing those thoughts and emotions, you are that much closer to unearthing your inner greatness. If you can learn to let go of the things holding you down in a low vibe state, you will quickly ascend through the emotional levels to your natural state, that of supreme bliss, and you will never look back.

Chapter Nine

MEDITATION, THE SINGLE MOST EFFECTIVE MENTAL TOOL IN YOUR ARSENAL

"The best cure for the body is a quiet mind"
– Napoleon Bonaparte

The average person has over six thousand thoughts each and every day, and this number can vary substantially depending on the individual and what they encounter on any given day, but whichever way you look at it, that is a lot of thoughts. I have previously compared the mind to a computer, and thoughts to tabs within an internet browser, now let's explore this concept a little more. Having an excessive number of tabs open on your computer's browser at any one time presents a host of problems.

- **Reduced computer performance.** The browser's ability to handle increased workloads depends on the machine's CPU speed and RAM size.
- **Decreased user efficiency.** The more tabs you have open, the less likely you are to return to them, and the more time that passes, the more likely you are to close them without reading them.
- **Increased stress.** Many tabs mean a cluttered browser and a cluttered mind. Each time you return to your browser, you make a mental note to start pouring over all of the pages you have earmarked to return to, this may sound trivial, but

you are without doubt burdening yourself unnecessarily, as you feel you must read these pages, for fear of missing out on what they may contain.

- **Reinforces a habit of not finishing things.** This is something I am particularly mindful of in my everyday life. Before, I would have opened a page I thought to be of particular interest, and I would have read the first couple of paragraphs and then think to myself, "That's very interesting, I'll come back to that later" which almost always resulted in me never coming back to it, as it would have been buried under many news subsequent pages. A new habit to consider is, read the page straight away, and if you don't have time right then, and you are convinced you will read it, then simply bookmark it and close it!

Until recent years, my mind was a mirror image of my phone's internet browser, needlessly cluttered and bogged down by countless thoughts, many of a negative or destructive nature. I did not become truly aware of the volume and nature of my thoughts until I discovered the miracle of meditation, and it is not an exaggeration to say that it has completely changed my life. Meditation was something I had heard about many times over the years, and many of the men I looked up to as role models attributed much of their success to meditation, including Arnold Schwarzenegger, Tony Robbins, Bruce Lipton, Joe Dispenza, Keanu Reeves and Will Smith to name just a few. It soon dawned on me that there must be something to this seemingly mystical practice.

At the age of twenty-five, I began meditating several times per week, for up to four or five weeks at a time, and looking back with fresh objective eyes, I can say that while I definitely benefitted from this newfound exercise, I did not do it enough to fully maximise the benefits. In the self-improvement world, there is a famous rule, the 21/90 rule. Although not an exact science, it is widely regarded that if you do something every day for twenty-one days, it will form a habit. If you continue to do it for ninety days, then it becomes a permanent lifestyle change. I meditated frequently enough for it to become a habit, but I did not make it over the ninety-day threshold until a few years later, at the age of twenty-eight, and that is when everything changed.

I was not consciously aware of when I passed the ninety-day threshold until several months later, at which point I reflected on the changes I had observed within myself. My mind had become predominantly calm, it was no longer the eternally spinning hamster wheel, pulling me down metaphorical rabbit holes numerous times a day. I had developed an unshakeable forcefield of calmness, which is fantastically useful each and every day of my life, such as on the congested commute to work in the morning, or if I encounter a particularly challenging patient or disgruntled customer, I am able to stay present, keep my ego in check and remain (almost) as still and calm as the surface of a pond.

Don't get me wrong, there are still many times where I feel a flame of anger or irritation flare up within me occasionally when something doesn't go quite right, but I am now much more aware of the thoughts in my head and the corresponding emotions in my body, and it is this awareness of them, that gives me the power to transmute them into peaceful presence. The ego (fear, anger, pride etc) cannot tolerate the intense light of consciousness, when you direct your attention towards it, they will dissolve within that light, leaving only blissful calm behind. The more you practice this, the easier it will become.

What is meditation?

"Most people assume that meditation is all about stopping thoughts, getting rid of emotions, somehow controlling the mind. But actually it's… about stepping back, seeing the thought clearly, witnessing it coming and going"

– Andy Puddicombe

There are several ways of describing meditation, but it is most popularly viewed as a technique for calming the mind, by temporarily halting the incessant stream of thought. Alternatively, it may be viewed as a means of paying attention to what is currently going on within your mind, this is called mindfulness. You are fully awake and alert, but the mind becomes clear and focused inwardly, rather than on the external world. The most comprehensive definition that I have uncovered so far is that provided by Indian yogi and author, Sadghuru.

"Meditation" or "Dhyana" means to go beyond the limitations of the physical body and the mind. Only when you transcend the limited perspective of the body and the mind do you have a complete dimension of life within you. When you are identified as the body, your whole life is only about survival. When you are identified as the mind, your whole perspective is enslaved to the social perspective, religious perspective, or the family perspective. You can't look beyond that. Only when you become free from the modifications of your own mind will you know the dimension of the beyond."

– Sadhguru

There are many different types of meditation available for you to try, here I have listed some of the most widely practiced today and I have included a very brief overview of each.

- **Mindfulness meditation** – Arguably one of the most

popular meditation techniques in the West today. With its origins in Buddhism, the aim is to acknowledge your thoughts as they enter your mind, but without judging them, or paying them any heed, you simply observe them as they enter, and let them pass on through. Think of mindfulness as watching luggage pass by on an airport conveyor belt, you see each and every bag pass by, but you do not go and claim any, but simply let them pass on. Like with thoughts, do not focus in on any one thought, rather, just let it pass on.
  - **Pros:** No teacher needed, easily practiced by yourself.
- **Transcendental meditation** – Another highly popular type of meditation today, it involves the use of a specially chosen mantra for the individual and is performed twice every day for twenty minutes.
  - **Cons:** You can only learn this style of meditation from a certified instructor, which can be quite expensive.
- **Spiritual meditation** – Similar to prayer practiced in Christianity, Hinduism, and Daoism, where you sit in silence, seeking a deeper and more profound connection with your God or the universe. Essential oils are often used to intensify the spiritual experience, including sandalwood, sage, frankincense, and myrrh.
- **Mantra meditation** – Prominent in Buddhism and Hindu traditions, the individual repeatedly utters a sound, or mantra over and over again, one of the most popular being "Om". This meditation is claimed to elevate alertness, provide deepened levels of awareness and brings the user closer into tune with the environment. This technique is especially suited for people who get antsy during periods of extended silence.
- **Visualisation meditation** – Possibly one of the most

individually customisable meditation styles available. This can involve you vividly imagining yourself achieving whatever it is you have your heart set on, or you can simply visualise positive or relaxing scenes, such as being in a beautiful forest on a spring day, or lounging on a Spanish beach, you are only limited by your imagination.

- **Movement meditation** – Ideal for people who find calm in action. Many activities can be suitable for this type of meditation, including yoga, qigong, walking through a forest, or even gardening to name a few.
- **Focused meditation** – Pick any one thing and focus on that, the breath cycle is a very popular one. Follow the air as it enters through the nose, passes down through the trachea and into the lungs, then reverse the process as you exhale. Another great way to do this technique is to simply stare at one thing, it can be a screw in a plain wall, or better yet, a candle flame. A great technique for increasing focus.
- **Progressive relaxation meditation** – aimed at progressively relieving tension in the body, this technique is also known as a body scan meditation. It can involve tightening and relaxing muscle groups throughout the body and can be effective in releasing stress and helping you to relax before bedtime.
- **Binaural beats meditation** – binaural beats have been used as a tool for meditation for a very long time. Today, they are most easily utilised by using headphones. Simply, they work by playing one fixed tone through one earpiece, and another slightly higher tone through the other ear, the brain creates a third tone, which is pitched at the difference between the two separate tones and aligns to that frequency. For example, if 10Hz is played through the left ear, and 20Hz

through the right ear, the difference is 10Hz, which as we know from chapter six, the brain, this frequency is within the alpha frequency bandwidth which is associated with super-learning and flow-state. They can be used to enhance a traditional meditative session, or they can be used in many other situations, such as when studying or when drifting off to sleep.

How to meditate

As outlined above, there are many different styles of meditation and techniques at your disposal, and as often happens in the digital age, there can be an overload of information available online when you perform a "how to meditate" Google search. To keep things as simple and practical as possible, I will share with you my personal recommendation on how to get started with your new meditation routine.

1. Find a quiet and secluded spot, this can be your living room, bedroom, car, a park bench or a remote nature location etc.
2. Play a simple soundtrack, I find nature sounds to be the most pleasant and unobtrusive. This can be via Youtube on your smart TV, phone, cd recording and can be played out loud or through headphones.
3. Set a countdown timer on your phone. Do not be overly ambitious to start off with, I would recommend five minutes for the first few sessions, once you get accustomed to finding the present moment and bringing your mind to a point of focus, you can then start increasing the duration.
4. Get comfortable, sitting, reclining, or lying down on the sofa or bed and close your eyes.
5. Listen to the sound in the recording, be it a babbling brook, the wind through the trees, the crackle of a fire, whatever

it may be. Listen to it without judgement, i.e. "That's a nice sound" because that by itself is thinking, which we are striving not to do! If and when any stray thoughts flash into your mind, acknowledge them, and let them pass on by. You are wanting to observe your thoughts and be aware of them, but not actively creating more of them. Breathe slowly and deeply throughout your meditation.

6. Alternatively, rather than focusing on the sounds in the nature scene, you can choose to simply focus on your breathing. Consciously inhale deeply and follow the flow of air into your lungs as they inflate, allowing your ribs to move upwards and outwards, then gently exhale, and visualise the air flowing out of the lungs, reversing the process, it should feel very smooth, easy, and relaxing.

What happens during meditation?

Generally speaking, and I say generally because what happens will vary slightly depending on what type of meditation you do, but for most meditations, the mind is brought to a singular focus, bra frequencies slow down and the tabs of your brain's internet browser close down one by one. You immerse yourself in the present moment.

"Meditation invokes that which is known in neuroscience as neuroplasticity, which is the loosening of the old nerve cells or hardwiring in the brain, to make space for the new to emerge."

– Craig Krishna

Benefits you may experience

At the end of the day, when studying any new technique, skill, practice or whatever it may be, I like many others want to know one thing above all others, and that is, how will this help me? Here I have outlined all of the major benefits of meditation that I have experienced personally, and ones that have been verified under scientific scrutiny.

- **Improved attention span and memory.** Published in the journal of Psychiatry Research in 2010, Harvard researchers found that undertaking an eight-week long program in mindfulness – based stress reduction resulted in increased concentrations of grey matter within the brain regions involved in learning, memory, emotion regulation, sense of self.
- **Reduced heartrate.** It was found that novice yoga practitioners were able to consciously reduce their heart rates by on average 10.7 beats per minute (bpm) after thirty days of yoga training, compared to a control group which showed no reduction in heart rate. A healthy heart rate is considered to range from approximately 60-100 bpm and allows the heart to maintain a healthy, steady rhythm, allowing it to keep plenty of energy in reserve to respond to daily stressors.
- **Reduced blood pressure and sense of calm.** The commonly accepted ideal blood pressure is 120/80, the top number being the systolic pressure, i.e., the blood pressure during contraction of the heart, and the bottom number representing the diastolic pressure, or the blood pressure during the relaxation phase of the heart-beat cycle. A study in the journal of Psychosomatic Medicine found that meditating for just ten minutes, twice per day was enough to lower systolic pressure by 2.7mmHg and diastolic pressure by 4.3mmHg compared to the non-meditation control group.

- **Reduction in pain.** In 2015, a research paper published in the Journal of Neuroscience demonstrated that mindfulness meditation significantly reduced the level of perceived pain for 75 healthy adults, more-so than the placebo effect or listening to a calming audiobook.
- **Reduced stress and inflammation.** One of the biggest problems in modern society, inflammation plays key roles in many diseases including, heart disease, diabetes, arthritis, and Crohn's disease to name just a few. Increased inflammation is caused by the production of inflammatory cytokine proteins and c-reactive protein, which work together to act as an early defence mechanism against injury and infection. Prolonged elevation of these inflammatory proteins gradually cripples the body's ability to heal and fight infection. Mindfulness meditation has been found to successfully reduce stress levels and subsequently the levels of pro-inflammatory proteins in the body.
- **Strengthened immune system.** Frequent meditation can boost the body's natural defences, specifically the white blood cells. We have two main types of white blood cells, killer-T cells which target and kill abnormal or damaged cells. The other type is B-lymphocytes, which produce antibodies, think of them as biological missiles, which seek and destroy foreign invading viruses and bacteria in addition to help with wound-healing and regulating homeostasis of the immune system within the body.
- **Reduced rate of ageing.** DNA, aka our genetic code is contained within chromosomes, and these chromosomes are tipped with telomere caps, think of these as like a shoelace cap. As we age, these telomere caps shorten over time. It has been discovered that chronic stress and depression can

substantially shorten these caps, making us age quicker as a result. Amazingly, it has been strongly suggested that regular meditation can preserve and even lengthen these caps, literally giving you a bit of your life back!
- **Improved quality of sleep.** Researchers at the University of Southern California observed that by following a mindfulness meditation routine for six weeks resulted in better quality sleep, significantly fewer sleep disturbances in addition to fewer sleep-related daytime disturbances such as mood fluctuations, anxiety, reduced attention span and clarity of thinking.
- **Improved mood, mental health and appreciation for life.** It is possible that these benefits may arise due to improved quality of sleep, they may also be due to the improved awareness of negative thoughts and stories present in your mind, which ultimately dissolves them, freeing you from their grasp.

As you can see from the list above, there is a tremendous number of potential benefits to be gained through meditation. Personally, I like to view meditation as a workout for the mind, albeit a passive one. Like training your body in the gym, growing mentally and spiritually through meditation takes time and commitment, but you will very likely begin to see changes not long into your journey. It is like most things in life, you get out what you put in.

Chapter Ten

GRATITUDE, SAYING THANK YOU GOES A LONG WAY

"Happiness cannot be travelled to, owned, earned, worn or consumed. Happiness is the spiritual experience of living every minute with love, grace, and gratitude."

– Denis Waitley

Compared to all of the tools laid out within the chapters of this book, I believe that this chapter contains the simplest and easiest practice to do, for two main reasons. The first reason is that being grateful for something comes naturally to every human being, or at least it should do, unless one has been overly spoiled from a very young age perhaps. The second reason is that the vast majority of people practice gratitude each and every day of their lives, possibly without even being aware of it.

Take a moment now and think back to a time in your childhood, or even adulthood, where you received something that meant a lot to you. It can be a material gift, it could be a date with your crush, or perhaps a dream job or even a promotion at work. Once you have selected the memory, recreate it in your mind with as much authenticity as you can, close your eyes and visualise what you saw, heard, smelt, tasted, felt. How did you feel at that precise moment in time? Generate the exact same emotions you felt in that precise moment in time and immerse yourself in them.

The key to this exercise is in recreating the sensation of gratitude that you felt when you received whatever it is you are thinking about. If you can successfully do this, you are flooding your mind, body and spirit with the emotion of gratitude, charging your entire being with positive energy and priming your body to receive before it has actually received in the physical world. When you are in a state of gratitude, it is impossible for you to feel bad, and any stress that might have been on your mind or in your body is immediately dissolved.

Have you ever stopped to take stock of things to be grateful for in your own life? If the answer is yes, then that's terrific! If the answer is no, then why not do it now? In the space below, write down ten things that you are grateful for in your life right now. You can even go a step further and include a reason why you are grateful for each thing.

I recommend starting each entry by writing "I am grateful for <INSERT ITEM/PERSON/ETC HERE> because <INSERT REASON HERE>.

Exercise 2 – Ten things that I am grateful for

1. ....
   ....
   ....

2. ....
   ....
   ....

3. ....

Feeling Great is your Natural State

....
....
4. ....
....
....
5. ....
....
....
6. ....
....
....
7. ....
....
....
8. ....
....
....
9. ....
....
....
10. ....
....
....

Gratitude has played and continues to play a large role in our history and civilisation. The American national holiday of Thanksgiving is a great example of an occasion established and focused on the act of gratitude. Another example is the Christian tradition of saying grace before every meal. All of the major religions have gratitude built into their fundamental principles, including Buddhism, Islam, Judaism and Hinduism. The Buddha taught that we have no cause for anything but gratitude and joy. Muhammad said that feeling gratitude for the abundance you have received is the best insurance that that abundance will continue.

A more common and perhaps relatable example can be found in everyday life. What do you do when paying for groceries at the till in your local supermarket and the cashier gives you your change? You say the magical words, "Thank you". When you start paying close attention to the things, opportunities and people that come into your life on a daily basis, or that are already a part of your life, you will soon see just how much you already have to be grateful for. A phrase that many people are painfully familiar with is "you don't know what you had until it's gone", and this is true for all things, health, wealth, relationships with friends, family or colleagues, a favourite breakfast cereal, etc. I will not list anymore, as I don't want to make preceding exercise too easy for you!

The more you think and say the words "thank you", the more gratitude you will generate and feel. The more gratitude that you feel, the better you feel and the more abundance you invite into your life. Stress will melt away, leaving behind only a blissful state of calmness. Isaac Newton's third law applies here just as much as it does in a high school physics exam question, in that for every action, there is an equal and opposite reaction, meaning that the more gratitude you feel and radiate outwards, the more you will receive in return. The exercise below is a simple, convenient and easy way of integrating more gratitude into your day.

EXERCISE 3A – GRATITUDE PRACTICE, A WALKING EXERCISE

When walking down the street, or from your car into work, or even when just taking the bins out on collection day, say the words "thank you" for every step that you take. The exact number does not matter, but the more the better. For example, if you have just parked your car and are walking to the ticket machine, if it is roughly eighty steps on each leg of the trip and you utter the magic words for every step, by the time you return to your car you will have given thanks at least one hundred and sixty times! It is a fantastic exercise which costs you nothing, and will only make you feel better, and more grateful for what you have in your life, while priming you to invite even more abundance into your life.

When you start to become more gratitude conscious, you make the switch from being in scarcity mode, where there is not enough money, goods or services for everyone in society, to being in a state of abundance, where you realise the truth, that there is in fact more than enough of everything for everyone. Another way of saying this is that you change from viewing the glass as half-empty, to half-full.

"When you arise in the morning think of what a privilege it is to be alive, to think, to enjoy, to love."

– Marcus Aurelius

I mentioned earlier that thoughts, and by extension images

and words are the language of the brain, or mind, and that feelings or emotions are the language of the body. There will come a point after consciously practicing the art of gratitude for a certain period of time where you will naturally feel it within you, all the time, like a permanent state of bliss or joy, as described earlier in the previous chapter. There is no set timeframe that this may happen within, it is entirely up to you, and how much of your time and energy you invest in it. A great way to reduce the time it takes to reach this point is to utilise what we know about the brain and its brainwaves, as discussed earlier in chapter six.

When you wake up in the morning, and just before you fall asleep at night, the brain is in its most malleable state, due to the predominance of theta brain waves. It is during these two windows that we are most susceptible to suggestion, or reprogramming, which is why it is so important for our mental health to avoid using social media or checking the news, as they are almost always negative experiences which lower your vibe, just ask yourself this, out of the last ten news bulletins to appear on your news app, how many of them were of a positive nature which taught you something useful or made you feel better than you did before reading it? So instead, let's use these bi-daily opportunities to start and end your day on a positive note.

Exercise 3b – Gratitude practice, a morning ritual

As soon as you wake up in bed, before you sit up, before you start thinking about the day ahead, say to yourself "thank you". Give thanks that you are alive, that you slept well (even if you didn't sleep well, act as if you did to simulate the feeling of gratitude) and have been blessed with another day of countless possibilities. This needn't take long, only a few minutes is enough to prime you for the great day ahead.

Exercise 3c – Gratitude practice, a bedtime ritual

When you are tucked up in bed and have just turned out the light with the intention of drifting off, as you feel sleep approach, think of all the things that happened to you during the day that you are grateful for and charge each one with pure and simple gratitude. Like with the morning routine, you do not need to spend an excessive amount of time on this, just enough to get you to the point where you are filled with thanks and appreciation for what you have in your life and all the good experiences that you had been gifted with that very day, they can be as simple as getting a great parking spot at work or being bought a cappuccino by a friend.

In the gospel of Matthew, he writes "whoever has will be given more, and they will have an abundance. Whoever does not have, even what they have will be taken from them." On the surface, this may sound selfish and problematic, such as in modern society where the rich become richer, and the poor become poorer. While this lesson may apply to material treasures, which is no bad thing by itself, if your desire is to accumulate riches, it also applies to love, joy and peace. Translated into real-life, if you go about life with little love in your heart, you will almost certainly repel people, including friends, family and any potential intimate relationships, just think of Scrooge in Dickens' Christmas Carol.

Conversely, if you go about your life with love and gratitude being the dominant forces or emotions within your heart, then you will without doubt only attract yet more of that same love into your life, in the form of close friendships, strengthened family bonds and pure eros love of the romantic kind, while simultaneously dissolving stress and transforming the way you view yourself and your life. It all starts with simply saying "thank you".

Chapter Eleven

THE LAW OF ATTRACTION: PART 1

> *"It is the law that determines the complete order in the universe, every moment of your life, and every single thing you experience in your life. It doesn't matter who you are or where you are, the law of attraction is forming your entire life experience, and this all-powerful law is doing that through your thoughts. You are the one who calls the law of attraction into action, and you do it through your thoughts."*
>
> – Rhonda Byrne, the Secret

In life, we don't get what we want, we get what we are. Whether you believe that you are lucky or unlucky, you are correct either way. As I have said earlier, your inner reality personality determines your outer reality, and in this chapter, we are going to shift our focus onto a concept known as the Law of Attraction.

The Law of Attraction is a product of the New Thought Movement, which is a spiritual movement originating in the United States of America in the early 1900s. I would also like to make clear that I will not be advocating one religion over another or arguing for or against the validity of any religious movement, I am rather providing some background information and context for the focal point of this chapter, which is the Law of Attraction itself.

New Thought holds several core beliefs. Firstly, it suggests that there is an infinite intelligence, or God essence permeating every atom, molecule, and area of space in the multiverse and is "supreme, universal and everlasting". The second belief is that divinity dwells within each and every person, that we are all eternal spiritual beings having a temporary human experience (a belief which mirrors that held by many of the larger mainstream religions). Thirdly, that the "highest spiritual principle is loving one another unconditionally" and finally that our mental state and the thoughts that we think are transmitted into the aether where they are picked up by infinite intelligence (or God) and later manifest as an experience in our daily lives.

There have been many books which focus on this spiritual philosophy, including the Science of getting Rich by Wallace Wattles published in 1910, Napoleon Hill's eternal classic Think and Grow Rich and more recently in 2006, the documentary The Secret by Rhonda Byrne was released, followed by a series of books further expanding on the original concept.

In the Bible, Matthew 7:7 we read (there is some variation between versions, but here we have the New International Version) "Ask and it will be given to you; seek and you will find; knock and the door will be opened to you". This is strikingly similar to what New Thought regards as the Law of Attraction, but it is suggested that the instructions in the bible are incomplete. Spiritualists, Yogis and Law of Attraction teachers and followers in general believe that for something to manifest in one's life, it is not enough to simply ask for it, there are two more key ingredients to the process. One is that you must visualise clearly what it is that you wish to manifest in your life, it could be the ideal body shape, a new job opportunity, your ideal bank balance possibly, or even a state of mind you wish to achieve. You are only limited by the scope of your imagination.

The second requirement is arguably the more difficult to fulfil but is still within reach of anyone willing to put the energy into it. You must feel like you already have that which you are asking for. The paradigm of most people today is that they can only be happy when they have a certain thing in their lives, only then will they allow themselves to feel joy, satisfaction, or gratitude. They are in effect externalising their happiness while projecting into the future, and directly saying to themselves and the universe, that the present moment is not good enough. This approach is akin to placing a metaphorical carrot in front of a metaphorical donkey, no matter how fast or for how long the donkey chases the carrot, it will never catch the carrot, because it is continuously ahead of the donkey, and just beyond grasp! When applying this metaphor to mindset and state of consciousness, see the flow-charts below.

It is extremely easy to fall into the paradigm of, "As soon as I am in a loving relationship, then I can go and do lots of things and visit places with them, then I will be happy". Instead, reverse the order of the previous statement to, "I will be happy now, in myself and do the things that I want to do and visit the places that I want to see, and it is only a matter of time before that loving relationship manifests". If your state of consciousness, i.e., love, joy or peace requires you to first acquire something to enable that feeling, then it will not last. Find that feeling within yourself first, cultivate it and everything else which comes into your life will compliment it and add to your own unshakable foundation.

[Once I have...] → [Then I can do...] → [Then I can be...]

[BE...] → [DO...] → [HAVE...]

Figure 2. The top process is the traditional train of thought, which when followed means that you can only achieve love, joy or peace through acquiring something beforehand.

The bottom process teaches the reverse; be how you want to be, then do what you want to do, then you can have what it is that you seek.

———

Wanting a positive experience in and of itself is actually a negative experience, because as far as the universe is concerned, you are broadcasting a signal of "lacking", but accepting a negative experience as it is, is in actuality a positive experience. Philosopher Alan Watts referred to this as "the backwards law" and we have touched upon its numerous times throughout this book so far, most recently with the carrot and the donkey. The more you pursue something, such as feeling better, the worse you will feel. This is because you are coming from a place of lacking, and if the universe gives us what we are, then you will receive more of that same lacking. If you want to have that ideal slim, strong, and healthy body, visualise what it would look like in your mind's eye. Picture yourself standing in front of the mirror, how lose your trousers' waistband feels on your waist. Generate the emotions you would experience if you had that perfect body. You might feel joy in looking how you want to look, you might feel self-love, peace, satisfaction, acceptance and optimism to name but a few.

Once you have an image of how you want to look, visualise and feel the desired future emotions, then you can BE happy (or any of the positive emotions listed earlier) then you will start taking action to realise the visualisation in your mind. This is a vital step in the process because the Law of Attraction is not a magical or mystical spell which produces results without you taking any action on your part. Taking action in this example could simply be having discipline when it comes to cleaning up your diet, which is substantially easier than you may think, owing to how much high-sugar artificial food we as a society consume on a daily basis.

Other actions might be taking cold showers, as outlined earlier, due to the fact that they promote conversion of metabolically inert white fat to calorie-burning brown fat, and that they also help to regulate your body's stress response, which reduces the amount of stress hormone, cortisol circulating in your blood at any given time, which will reduce the amount of excess fat being stored in your body. And more obviously, action could also take the form of attending the gym or exercise classed on a regular basis. Once you start doing these things and DO them consistently (that was not an exhaustive list of potential actions to take, but just some of the key ones in my opinion), you will eventually manifest and HAVE your desired body!

You are creator

The law of attraction is not limited in what it can do. The only limitations are set by you, specifically by what you can imagine and what you believe is possible. If it is fortune you seek, quantify it. How much do you want or need? Most people cannot answer this question, but if you take the time, sit down with a pen, paper and calculator, work out exactly how much it is you need to either purchase that car of your dreams, that trip of a lifetime, or even how much you would need to retire from your job and sail off into the sunset.

Once you have arrived at the number, write it down on a card or piece of paper. There are any number of ways that you can word this, and there is no right or wrong way to frame it, but personally I recommend you keep it simple and concise, for example, "I intend to acquire no less than £5000 within the next 12 months". By including a timeframe, i.e., 12 months, you substantially improve your chances of manifesting what it is you seek, because with no time-parameter, the request or goal is open-ended, you could perhaps liken it to posting a letter without a stamp.

After writing this statement down, place it somewhere you will see it every day, such as on your bedside table or perhaps on the wall facing your bed. Look at it every morning, first thing. Visualise the money in your bank account, or investment portfolio, simulate the feelings and emotions you would experience if it was suddenly there right now, hold onto this feeling and savour it for several minutes, thanking the universe that your desire has been manifested, then let it go and think no more of it for the rest of the day. Simply, set it and forget it. One of the amazing aspects of this process is that you do not need to consciously find a way to manifest your goal, rather, the means will flash into your mind as a moment of inspiration, an "Aha!" moment. It is then your responsibility to act on these instructions, or inspiration as soon as possible, otherwise the idea will pass onto someone who will capitalise on it.

In the book Think and Grow Rich, the author goes into some detail as to how this works, although he does not specifically mention the Law of Attraction, he was alluding to exactly the same process, albeit worded slightly differently. Hill describes the brain as both a transmitting and receiving station, in direct contact with infinite intelligence. Infinite intelligence has been described to be akin to an invisible cosmic database call, referred to as the Akashic Records by theosophists, which each and every one of us has the potential to tap into. Others view this infinite intelligence as God, or simply universal intelligence. Call it what you will, but this cosmic database inhabits a higher dimension from the one that we humans exist within, and is essentially a complete library of every thought, idea, action and event that has ever happened in the past, present or future.

When you hold an image in your mind of what you want, such as gaining an answer to a problem, or a way to complete a certain task, you transmit into the aether your desire for the answer to your question, but you must do so in a spirit of unwavering faith. Your request must be charged with the emotion of faith, in that you believe you will receive what you ask for. Your request will be picked-up by this infinite intelligence and returned to you in the form of a solution to your problem. The solution will be received by the subconscious mind, which will at some point present itself to the conscious mind in the form a hunch, or divine inspiration.

Some of my experiences with the law of attraction

For a long time, I had many demons living inside my head. Up to my early-mid-twenties when I discovered the world of self-development, I carried a large amount of bitterness and lack of direction in my life. Throughout my first time at university and for some time afterwards, I was directionless, which led to a chronic sense of frustration at not knowing what to do with my life, bitterness that others were getting ahead and at times resentment towards myself and others in my life.

It was not until I was 24 and working a job I did not want to be in within the civil service, when I had a major epiphany. This sudden flash of divine intervention told me that I should return to university to study optometry, to become an optometrist. Suddenly, everything seemed to be 6/6 (20/20 if you are in America) and crystal clear, I finally knew what I wanted to do in life and had the will to act on it. Fast-forward several years later, when I was helping my mum with moving home, at this point I had already graduated from Optometry school, I came across a box with a stash of my old schoolbooks and folders. As chance would have it, I found my old careers study journal from when I was in junior school.

After blowing almost one and a half decades-worth of dust off the cover, I cracked it open and proceeded to flick through the pages. There was not much in it, but several pages in, I saw something which literally leapt off the page to me. The page was titled "10 jobs I like". This was dated October 2004, which would have made me thirteen years old, in second year of grammar school. I will not bore you with the entire list, but needless to say that some of the most typical early-teen choices were on it, including, doctor, astronaut and world-class jazz trumpeter, the usual careers! These entries did not shock me, what shocked me was that at the top of the list, my thirteen-year-old self had written "optometrist". This discovery gave me goosebumps. Without even knowing it at the time, I had successfully manifested my childhood ambition over fourteen years after first setting the intent, yes, it took longer than I would have perhaps liked it to, but the universe and infinite intelligence do not follow our ideal timeframes, as time is a man-made construct, devised by us to help us go about our lives.

Taking some time to pause and reflect over many aspects of my life, in hindsight the law of attraction has been acting continuously, for both good and bad. It needs to be said now that the law is a double-edged sword, or two sides of the same coin. While you can manifest good into your life, you can also manifest bad. Let me give you several favourable examples where the law has provided me with exactly what I sought.

A MIRACULOUS RECOVERY

When I was living at home while I studied to become an optometrist, a stray cat appeared outside our window one day. It was a small, but sturdy looking beast, and due to circumstances at the time, she was not allowed into the house, so declared my father. Fast forward several months and the little critter had evolved from being a random stray lurking in the shadows of the rhododendron bushes, to becoming an integral member of the family. We gave her the name Cilla, because she was mostly covered in black fur, and my step mum made a link between this and a famous British TV presenter, Cilla Black, in hindsight it was the most obvious name in the world!

The age-old question of which are better, cats or dogs is

an extremely polarising topic of conversation, one which has both forged and destroyed relationships across the world and throughout the ages. Personally, my preference has leaned towards our canine friends, because they are exactly that, our friends. You know exactly where you stand with a dog, as they have the either the ability and/or decency to convey emotion, but not so much with felines. A cat could be sleeping peacefully on your lap one moment, then at the drop of a hat it can be embedding its preposterously sharp claws into your delicate and tender skin. Cilla breaks the mould, however.

Cilla is a cat, with a personality comprising approximately 80% dog and 10% housecat and 10% apex predator. She is doglike in that she will get up off her resting place to come and greet you when you return home after being away for even just a few hours. Furthermore, she gets visibly excited when you step near the fridge, as she knows that the fridge contains sliced ham, and it is an understatement to say that she loves ham, as she will literally jump in the air to swipe it from your outstretched hand. On the other hand, Cilla is slightly cat-like in her personality in that she sleeps, a lot, and can appear quite indifferent to things at times, unlike dogs, which almost always give away their emotions.

Thirdly, Cilla is part apex predator, because more often than not, there will be a small gift left neatly just outside the back door of the house, usually in the form of an unfortunate rodent, or a small bird. We believe that these are gifts presented by Cilla as her way of proving her worth to the household, or maybe she simply likes showing off, we may never know for sure!

In late March 2021, Cilla broke her back right femur. My dad suspected something was seriously wrong when she would not come out of her little house just outside the back door. He eventually managed to extract her from the house by pulling out the entire rug lining the structure with her on it, and he could see right away that something was badly wrong with one of her back legs, as it was sitting in an extremely unnatural position, and the poor thing was clearly in a great deal of pain.

Fast forward twenty-four hours, and the vet had just given my dad and step mum a tough choice. Either pay several thousand pounds for surgery to fix the leg, with no guarantee of a great outcome, amputate the leg, of put her to sleep. I was at work when my dad called me to tell me all of this. I will keep this as concise as necessary and simply say that we opted to have the leg amputated, and the procedure was a success, or so we thought.

Cilla was brought home after twenty-four hours of observation and seemed to be on the mend, but within two days of returning home, it soon became apparent that something was not right. She was refusing to eat, which was completely out of character for her, and she was extremely lethargic, which is understandable, as she had just been through a horrific ordeal and was probably still in a state of prolonged shock or confusion. After several days of no change, my step-mum insisted on taking her back to the vets, who soon determined that Cilla was in fact severely jaundiced, and there may have been some additional issues, but nothing that the vet could detect. There was also a chance that she was losing the will to live.

My brother in particular was quite distressed by this, more than I thought he would be if truth be told, but people react differently in different situations. Regardless, I decided to consciously use the law of attraction to help Cilla. I knew that she was not "going to" make a full recovery, because she was already "making" a full recovery. I gave thanks for her perfect health. For fifteen minutes I meditated on the images and feelings of her restored to her old previous self, the visualisation was as clear as day, and I made it feel as real as possible. Once I had finished, I simply let it go from my mind and did not think about it for the rest of the day. The following day I was informed by my dad that Cilla had made what seemed like a miraculous recovery, overnight. To which I replied, "I know".

You may view this as simple chance, luck or coincidence, but I know that this was the result of sending a clear message to the universe, charged with gratitude and backed by an unwavering sense of faith that what I was asking was being fulfilled. Either way, I am sure Cilla doesn't mind, she is probably just happy to be back on rodent-patrol!

The most persistent wart in the world

Typically speaking, I have had very few skin problems in my life so far, apart from the occasional allergy-related rash and the rare appearance of a small wart or two. In March of 2020, a small wart appeared on the edge of my right hand's palm, so I did what any man would do, and simply ignore it, assuming it would miraculously resolve by itself. Unfortunately, this cunning strategy did not work, as the wart grew slightly larger over the next few weeks. It was at this point that I resolved to act and purchased an over-the-counter anti-wart kit.

The kit consisted of a viscose gel to be applied nightly, which when dry would form a thin but solid coating over the wart, killing it slowly over time. An emery board was also included in this kit, which was to be used to file this layer down, and taking the wart with it, one small layer at a time. I had previously purchased this kit numerous times over the previous few years, to resounding successes each time, usually taking no longer than two weeks to completely eradicate the presence of any wart. This time however, the wart did not retreat from whence it came, it persisted, for 6 months!

For 6 months, I applied the gel and filed it down to the point where there was nothing left but smooth, flat skin, but it returned, over and over again. Frankly speaking, it was not annoying enough for me to consider visiting the GP to request having it frozen and removed, so I decided to consciously put the law of attraction to the ultimate test, of fixing this tenacious wart.

My morning routine consists of a cold shower, followed by three rounds of the breathing routine outlined in chapter two, which takes around fifteen minutes to complete, I then spend some time setting my intentions for the day and beyond that.

One morning when setting my intentions, I included healing my wart in my list. For several uninterrupted minutes, I pictured my hand without the wart, I felt the relief and gratitude of it having resolved and immersed myself in that experience, holding onto it for several minutes, before simply letting it go and moving on with my intention list. I continued with my routine of applying the anti-wart gel and filing it down, I did not change my treatment routine in any way whatsoever, but before the end of the week, it was completely healed and for the first time in half a year, did not recur! You may argue that it was simply a coincidence that it should heal the same week I utilised the Law of Attraction, but the "how" is not what matters with this law, only the end result.

Chapter Twelve

THE LAW OF ATTRACTION: PART 2

Birds of a feather flock together

In the 2006 classic, the Secret, there is a law of attraction exercise which the reader is encouraged to try, and that is simply attracting a feather, but not just any feather, rather, a feather with a very particular colour, design or texture. Naturally, I obliged and performed the exercise myself, with a somewhat sceptical mind too, as this was the first time, I had ever attempted anything remotely as esoteric as this.

I pictured in my mind a long, slender, blue and white feather. The colours were distinct, with one half of the feather being completely white, and the other half a bright royal blue. I held the image in my mind's eye for a short time, I imagined the feeling I would experience if I were to actually see this feather with my eyes open, I then let the image and feeling go and forgot about it. Several days later, I had almost completely forgotten about the feather, until one evening when I happened to be scrolling through the comment section of a Youtube video, as fate would have it, I saw my feather, exactly how I had imagined it!

I had assumed that it would manifest for me in the physical world, but instead it had appeared in the digital world. This might be because I was not specific enough when sending my intension out to the infinite intelligence of the universe, perhaps

I should have generated the feeling of physically holding the feather, but regardless, I was quite speechless, because I had never seen a feather like this before, other than in my mind's eye when I visualised it.

After taking time to reflect on both the major and minor occurrences throughout my life with an objective and analytical lens, I can see many more examples of where the law of attraction played its role, but at the time, I was completely ignorant of it. Every person, experience, job, item etc has manifested for better or worse, completely as the result of my habitual thinking, or thought patterns, or in other words, the things I would think to myself, and the stories I would tell myself on a daily basis.

Try it for yourself

Before you come to any conclusions, why not try the method for yourself? Pick something simple and definite, such as a cappuccino, or the aforementioned feather. First picture the item, experience, or opportunity that you want to manifest in your life, clearly in your mind, charge it with a positive emotion such as faith, love, joy or gratitude and simply intend for it to come into your life. For example, "I intend to receive a cappuccino free of charge in the near future" while picturing the steaming hot liquid being poured into the cup, the smell of the coffee beans in the air, the flavour of the sweet, caffeinated goodness flowing down your throat and the gratitude you experience in receiving it. Immerse yourself in the experience before you have experienced it, you must align yourself on the frequency of having what it is you seek, rather than the frequency of wanting it, which is coming from a place of lacking.

After you have done all of this, forget about it, and leave it up to the universe, God or fate, whichever you prefer. Remember, simply set it then forget it. When consciously utilising this law, it is not up to you to figure out the means by which you reach your goal, because if you set the intention to the universe in a spirit of faith or charged with any of the positive emotions for that matter, you will eventually receive the inspiration or answer that you seek, the ball is then in your court, and it is your responsibility to act on it. Using the cappuccino example, it could appear in the form of your manager buying a round of coffees for the whole team, or you may be gifted a voucher by a satisfied customer with whom you had previous dealings with.

This is certainly not what many would call conventional thinking, but this may also explain why the overwhelming majority of people are not living the lives that they would like to. If you want to be happy, successful, free of stress or simply live a life of meaning, you first have to think thoughts which align with that goal, constantly, in a spirit of faith where they are charged with a positive emotion as mentioned earlier. You have absolutely nothing to lose by tapping into this power, but you do have everything to gain.

COINCIDENCE OR SYNCHRONICITY?

In many professions, it is usually a requirement to complete a period of supervised practice. In the UK optometry world, this period is called the pre-registration, or pre-reg year. Throughout this period, there is a substantial number of hoops to jump through, of which I will not bore you to tears with, but suffice to say, it is a very tough year for any newly graduated optometrist. It took me a long time to fully find my rhythm and start consistently and accurately applying everything I had learned at university, in fact, I reached a point after what was without doubt the worst assessment I had ever had in my life, where I considered throwing in the towel and calling it quits. Up to this point in my life, I had done countless exams, presentations and assessments of all kinds, having completed three university degrees, and I knew how to study, and study well. Despite all of my academic experience and determination, I could not find my flow.

I was not fully aware of it at the time, but up to this point in my pre-reg year, I had been completely neglecting my mental and more importantly, spiritual well-being. It soon became apparent when I paused to self-reflect, that I was living in a state of chronic stress, and at the time of that particular assessment it had begun manifesting as crippling stomach pains, which I had never ever experienced prior to that point, they persisted for several weeks. After looking at myself in the metaphorical mirror, I soon realised that this way of living could not continue, as it was killing me slowly.

Fortunately, I was able to become aware of this before it was too late. I began meditating daily again and practiced mindfulness throughout the day, constantly monitoring my thoughts and staying present to the moment, which prevented my mind from creating hypothetical worst-case scenarios which I can gladly say, ultimately never came to pass! I also owe much of my transformation to the breathing routine discussed in chapter two and frequent cold exposure, which substantially increased my tolerance to stress.

Additionally, for a period of 30 days, I followed a gratitude routine, which we have looked at in chapter ten. In less than a week of commencing meditation, cold exposure and gratitude practices, everything had changed, the stomach pains had ceased, I was sleeping substantially better, my mind did not create hypothetical stressful scenarios, and I could enter flow-state, much more easily and more often than I had been able to previously. After the 30-day gratitude routine was completed, I found myself being more grateful for everything that I had in life, from having a box of cereal in the kitchen cupboard, to the great health I was experiencing and still do experience every single day. Every one of the techniques or practices described within these pages is powerful in its own right, but when they are added together, their effects compound substantially, more and more overtime.

Like attracts like

Have you ever known someone who repeatedly did what you would consider to be bad things, and never received justice for them? Whereas you may have found yourself receiving a dose of karmic justice for a small slight which you committed at some point along the path of life and thought, "Why am I being punished for this when there are so many worse people in the world doing worse things than me?" Maybe you have pondered on this at some point, maybe not, but the key message here is that we are not punished for our sins, but we are punished by our sins.

This is an extremely important concept to understand because you don't receive in life what you want, but instead you receive what you are. For example, if you peak at your classmate's answers during a university test, and later feel guilty about this transgression, that guilt substantially lowers your level of vibration, which in turn will attract more occurrences into your life of the same vibration level, like-attracts-like. There are numerous ways to prevent this from happening, the first and foremost being, study well and don't cheat in a university test!

The second way of freeing yourself from this low-vibe prison is to confess to your colleague about what you did, and apologise, therefore absolving yourself of any guilt that you will be feeling. The third way is to simply let go of the guilt. When you let go of a negative emotion, you will naturally rise up to a higher emotional state, or level of consciousness, which is where the magic happens.

Reality is like playdough

The limits of what you can attract into your life are set entirely by you, and the thoughts which you think day-in and day-out, which ultimately form the basis of the stories that you tell yourself. Your personality and outer reality are the products of your inner reality. I grew up believing myself to be shy and lacking confidence, but that view has changed substantially over the years. I now feel completely comfortable being the centre of attention, occasionally, and in the right situation, such as if I'm playing a particularly competitive game of bowling! I am yet to score a perfect 300, my current record being a somewhat respectable 226, but the perfect game will manifest itself eventually, of that I have no doubt.

I do not crave being the centre of attention, but I am comfortable receiving the attention and mingling with new people. I reached this point over time, where I gained more experience in interacting with more and more varied people, but more importantly, I started seeing myself as a sociable person, who could talk to anyone, and now I can, and do! Simply put. Change your thoughts, change how you see yourself, change your reality.

When I look back over the years and compare who I

associated with then to who I do now, there have been some interesting changes. There were certain individuals who led self-destructive lives, but because I had known them for so long throughout school, that I may have been blinded to it, and in turn I developed some of those traits myself, such as excessive drinking on Saturday nights, slacking off on my studies and generally not channelling my energy into more constructive avenues. People will always come and go in each of our lives, a fact we are all familiar with, but who you surround yourself with has a huge impact on your reality. When did you last take stock of your immediate circle? Do you have common interests? Do you have similar goals in life? Do their beliefs and values align with yours?

Ever since I started becoming aware of my thoughts and who I have in my life, I started becoming much more aware of what I was thinking and selective about who I let into my immediate circle. I found myself no longer wanting to associate with "glass half empty" people, as I found their low frequency vibes and pessimistic outlooks did not serve me and in actuality, lowered my own vibe. I now make an effort to associate with optimistic, open-minded, happy people with a desire to constantly develop and better themselves. I quickly came to learn that there are comparatively few people who meet these criteria, but I would rather have a small number of people in my network who resonate with me and I with them, who push each other to continually level up and be the best that they can be, physically, emotionally, spiritually or financially.

To summarise, this is not the sort of material that is taught in schools, because of the value and power it provides to each individual, and also because it does not follow the dogmatic paradigm recognised by the majority within modern society, but that does not diminish its relevancy to your life in anyway whatsoever. In order to make the law of attraction really work for you, the way that you want it to, you will need to first let go of all attachments holding you down in a low emotional state.

Let go of stress, let go of the self-limiting beliefs and the stories that you currently tell yourself. Realise that you are not your mind, nor are you ruled by your mind, but instead, you are a divine conscious awareness having a temporary human experience. When you can do all of this, you will naturally and effortlessly rise to an elevated state of consciousness. In these higher states of consciousness, you will see things in a completely new light. You will see abundance everywhere, rather than scarcity. You will see and experience love, rather than hate. You will have finally come to realise the truth, that feeling great really is your natural state.

Final thoughts

I remember years ago when in our early teens, my brother and I would spend some time playing video games, we were not avid gamers by any stretch of the imagination, but we still enjoyed a decent first-person shooter as much as the next guy! One game which we played quite a lot was Grand Theft Auto: Vice City, which was a third person, open-world style game, where you had free roam across an entire city, you could complete main and side-quests, buy clothes, drive cars, helicopters and even boats. You had the option of solely sticking to the objectives of the game, or you could deviate from the set path and simply cause carnage across the city, in many different ways.

With this game there were many different cheat codes which you utilise if you desired, including invulnerability to bullets, erasing your character's wanted level by the city's police department, the ability to spawn supercars and superbikes anywhere, anytime. It was also possible to spawn a tank, a literal combat-capable, armoured tank. A separate cheat code was available which enabled vehicles to fly once enough speed had been accumulated, and in the case of the tank, it could fly indefinitely, if you utilised the canon effectively as a means of propulsion. My brother and I spent many a Sunday afternoon flying a Panzer tank over the streets of Vice City, all the while causing carnage where we went! Why you ask? Because we could.

The cheat codes enabled us to be like gods, within the game. We could essentially do whatever we wanted, with little to no repercussions, and even if there were, such as the city's SWAT team storming in after our characters, we could simply input another cheat code which would erase our criminal records. As fun as this was, the allure of unbridled power eventually faded, and all that was left was boredom and lack of direction, as we had completed the game's main objectives, we were essentially drifters within the game's city.

Free reign without consequences became boring because there was no resistance to our will. As humans, we need resistance in our lives in order to gain meaning, satisfaction, and to keep us moving forward. A life without resistance is like a bicycle whose chain has come off the sprocket, it's incredibly easy to turn the pedals, but that action does not move you forward, like it did when the chain was still attached. On the other hand, too much resistance is clearly harmful, and can lead to chronic stress, frustration, bitterness, anxiety, depression or even worse for some individuals.

The tools outlined in this book are not magical silver bullets which will solve all of the problems in your life overnight. They will not ensure that only good things come your way either. What these tools do however is still unimaginably useful and beneficial for you. Each and every chapter contains relevant and actionable knowledge and advice which when utilised consistently will transform how you view yourself, how you view your life and how you view other people. These tried and tested methods will increase your tolerance to the adversities and stressors you face on a daily basis. You will no longer be a victim of your environment, or of the incessant chatter that is your mind.

If you master all of the methods we have explored within these pages, you will be more confident in your work, or at home, or even simply out in the street, this increased confidence will result in increased competence, which will further reinforce your elevated confidence in a positive feedback loop. You will be like a rock in a raging river, where you are aware of the chaos in the world around you, but as you now have the ability to stay present, maintaining a calm and focused mind, you shall not be moved and carried away in the torrent of modern life. Your health, both physical and mental will be greater than it was before, which in turn will only increase your gratitude for what you have in life, which will ultimately attract more and more abundance into your life, each and every day.

Michelangelo did not sculpt his David in a day, but over three years of intense labour. He began with nothing more than a large lump of marble, which he transformed into a seventeen-foot-tall representation of the biblical King. Interestingly, Michelangelo claimed that he did not create the final masterpiece, rather he saw it within the marble and simply set it free. I like to think that we are all like that original lump of marble. Each of us has greatness within, in ways we may never have imagined, all you need to do is find it, and set it free. To do that, simply start implementing the tools outlined within these pages and see for yourself.

"I saw the angel in the stone, and I carved until I set it free."
– Michelangelo

Self-improvement is not a linear process, much like an index fund in the stock market, which can go up or down on any given day, week, month or year, you may at times feel like you are regressing or just staying the same, but if you persevere and stay the course, like with an index fund, over time your results will compound. Eventually, some day you will look back on how you used to be weeks, months or even years ago, and you will see clearly through the lens of hindsight, just how much you have evolved, but most importantly, you will have come to realise that the source of pure, unadulterated happiness really is attainable, because it is within you, it always has been, and it always will be.

BIBLIOGRAPHY

Anon. (2020). *Mental health statistics.* Available: https://mhfaengland.org/mhfa-centre/research-and-evaluation/mental-health-statistics/#anxiety. Last accessed 23rd Dec 2020.

Anon. (2020). *What is Neuroplasticity?* Available: https://brainworksneurotherapy.com/what-neuroplasticity. Last accessed 15th Dec 2020.

Anon. (2019). *Neuroplasticity: the potential for lifelong brain development.* Available: https://sharpbrains.com/resources/1-brain-fitness-fundamentals/neuroplasticity-the-potential-for-lifelong-brain-development/. Last accessed 12th Dec 2020.

Barnes, V. Davis, H. Murzynowski, J. Treiber, F. (2004). Impact of meditation on resting and ambulatory blood pressure and heart rate in youth. *Psychosomatic medicine.* 66 (6), 909-914.

Black, D. Slavich, G. (2016). Mindfulness meditation and the immune system: a systematic review of randomized controlled trials. *Academic science.* 1373 (1), 13-24.

Breus, M. (2018). *Can Intermittent Fasting Help Sleep?* Available: https://thesleepdoctor.com/2018/12/18/can-intermittent-fasting-help-sleep/. Last accessed 2nd Dec 2020.

Byrne, R (2006). *The Secret.* New York: Simon and Schuster.

Byrne, R (2012). *The Magic.* New York: Simon and Schuster.

Chetelat, G. Lutz, A. Marchant, N. (2018). Why could meditation practice help promote mental health and well-being in aging? *Alzheimer's Research & Therapy.* 10 (57), 1-2.

Cypess, A. Kahn, C. (2010). Brown fat as a therapy for obesity and diabetes. *Current Opinion Endocrinol Diabetes*

Obesity. 17 (2), 143-149.

Dickens, C (1843). *A Christmas Carol.* England: Chapman and Hall.

Dispenza, J. (2017). The present moment. In: *Becoming Supernatural.* London: Hay House. 27-60.

Eagleman, D. (2007). *10 Unsolved Mysteries of The Brain.* Available: https://www.discovermagazine.com/mind/10-unsolved-mysteries-of-the-brain. Last accessed 7th Dec 2020.

Epel, E. Daubenmier, J. Moskowitz, J. Folkman, S. Blackburn, E. (2009). Can meditation slow rate of cellular aging? Cognitive stress, mindfulness, and telomeres. *Academic Science.* 1172 (1), 34-53.

Galva, V. Jin, K. (2007). Neurogenesis in the aging brain. *Clinical Interventions in Aging.* 2 (4), 605-610.

Garcia-Rill, E. (2009). Reticular Activating System. In: *Encyclopaedia of Neuroscience.* Arkansas: Academic Press. 137-143.

Gard, T. Holzel, B. Lazar, S. (2014). The potential effects of meditation on age-related cognitive decline: a systematic review. *Annals of the New York Academy of Sciences.* 1307 (1), 89-103.

Hawkins, D. (2002). Levels of human consciousness. In: *Power vs Force.* Croydon: Hay House. 97-114.

Hill, N. (1937). The mystery of sex transmutation. In: *Think and grow rich.* New York: Penguin Group. 205-208.

Holzel, B. Carmody, J. Vangel, M. Congleton, C. Yerramsetti. Gard, T. Lazar, S. (2011). Mindfulness practice leads to increases in regional brain grey matter density. *Psychiatry research.* 191 (1), 36-43.

Knurek, S. (2018). *Understanding cortisol, the stress hormone.* Available: https://www.canr.msu.edu/news/understanding_cortisol_the_stress_hormone. Last accessed 14th Nov 2020.

Kox, M. Eijk, L. Zwaag, J. Wildenbery, J. Sweep, F. Hoeven, J. Pickkers, P. (2014). Voluntary activation of the sympathetic nervous system and attenuation of the innate immune response in humans. *Proc Natl Acad Sci USA.* 111 (20), 7379-7384.

Lu, S. (2014). *How chronic stress is harming our DNA.* Available: https://www.apa.org/monitor/2014/10/chronic-stress. Last accessed 18th Nov 2020.

Mattson, M. Moehi, K. Ghena, N. Schmaedick, M. Cheng, A. (2018). Intermittent metabolic switching, neuroplasticity and brain health. *Nat Rev Neurosci.* 19 (2), 63-80.

Nestler, E. Barrot, M. Self, D. (2001). ΔFosB: A sustained molecular switch for addiction. *Proc Natl Acad Sci USA.* 98 (20), 11042–11046.

Pandyna, S. (2011). Understanding Brain, Mind and Soul: Contributions from Neurology and Neurosurgery. *Men's Sana Monographs.* 9 (1), 129-149.

Rynders, C. Thomas, E. Zaman, A. Pan, Z. Catenacci, V. Melanson, E. (2019). Effectiveness of Intermittent Fasting and Time-Restricted Feeding Compared to Continuous Energy Restriction for Weight Loss. *Nutrients.* 11 (10), 2442.

Shanebrook, J. (2017). *Whole Body Cryotherapy: A Long-Term Weight/Fat Loss Method.* Available: https://chillcryotherapy.net/whole-body-cryotherapy-a-long-term-weightfat-loss-method/. Last accessed 27th Nov 2020.

Tanaaz (2020). *Understanding the 3 States of Consciousness: 3D, 4D, and 5D.* Available: https://foreverconscious.com/

understanding-3-states-consciousness-3d-4d-5d. Last accessed 29th Nov 2020.

Tosini, G. Ferguson, I. Tsubota, K. (2016). Effects of blue light on the circadian system and eye physiology. *Molecular Vision*. 22 (1), 61-72.

Tolle, E. (1999). Moving deeply into the now. In: *The Power of Now*. 2nd ed. United Kingdom: Yellow Kite. 50-51.

Tolle, E. (2008). Consciousness. In: *Oneness with all life*. Great Britain: Penguin Random House. 119-140.

Varady K.A., Bhutani S., Klempel M.C., Kroeger C.M. Comparison of effects of diet versus exercise weight loss regimens on LDL and HDL particle size in obese adults. Lipids Health Dis. 2011; 10:119. doi: 10.1186/1476-511X-10-119.

Vera. (2016). *3D, 4D and 5D – The Dimensions and their Differences*. Available: https://thewakeupexperience.eu/3d-4d-and-5d-the-dimensions-and-their-differences/. Last accessed 29th Nov 2020.

Williams, M. (2015). Prepare. In: *Do Breathe: Calm Your Mind. Find Focus. Get Stuff Done*. London: The do book company. 13-23.

Wu, R. Liu, L. Zhu, H. Su, W. Cao, Z. Zhong, S. Liu, X. Jiang, C. (2019). Brief Mindfulness Meditation Improves Emotion Processing. *Frontiers in Neuroscience*. 13 (1), 1074.

Zeidan, F. Emerson, N. Farris, S. Ray, J. Jung, Y. McHaffie, J. Coghill, R. (2015). Mindfulness Meditation-Based Pain Relief Employs Different Neural Mechanisms Than Placebo and Sham Mindfulness Meditation-Induced Analgesia. *The journal of neuroscience*. 35 (46), 15307-15325.

Printed in Great Britain
by Amazon